GAIL VAZ-OXLADE'S
RETIREMENT
ANSWER BOOK

CY2{

GAIL VAZ-OXLADE'S
RETIREMENT
ANSWER BOOK

Second Revised Edition

Published in 1997 by
Stoddart Publishing Co. Limited
34 Lesmill Road
Toronto, Canada
M3B 2T6
Tel. (416) 445-3333
Fax (416) 445-5967

01   00   99   98   97   1   2   3   4   5

Canadian Cataloguing in Publication Data

Vaz-Oxlade, Gail E., 1959–
The retirement answer book

2nd rev. ed.
Includes index.
ISBN 0-7737-5860-7

1. Retirement income – Planning.   2. Finance, Personal.
3. Retirees – Finance, Personal.   I. Title.

HD7129.V395 1997   332.024'01   C97-930337-0

Cover design: Pekoe Jones/*multiphrenia*

Printed and bound in Canada

CONTENTS

THANKS Y'ALL

Several people helped me by taking time out of their busy lives to review the manuscript. Thanks to Dave Frankham, Angela Koth, and Barbara Young. You'll see your ideas have been incorporated.

Thanks to my Mom and Dad, who have always stood firmly behind me, telling me that I'm the greatest! This one's for you guys.

And thanks to Kenny, my husband, whom I rely on for his soft honesty and enduring patience.

Gail E.

INTRODUCTION

retire 1: to withdraw from action or danger: retreat **2**: to withdraw esp. for privacy **3**: to fall back: recede **4**: to withdraw from one's position or occupation: conclude one's working or professional career
Webster's New Collegiate Dictionary

When you hear the word "retirement," what do you think of? The closing of one chapter and the opening of another? New opportunities and challenges? Or boredom, lethargy, and a withdrawal from life? Many people see retirement as an ending. But I believe retirement is an opportunity for new beginnings — a *restyling* of life — during which we can do more of what we *want* to do, as opposed to what we *have* to do.

Retirement used to have the image of being the "best time of our lives." That image has been blown apart by the reality that, for many people, with retirement comes illness, poverty, and loneliness. But it doesn't have to be that way. To have a successful retirement, we have to plan. After all, if you want to be successful at just about anything, some planning is required. We know that successful marriages and fulfilling parenthood don't just come naturally. They take hard work, persistence, and a commitment to doing it right. And retirement — the next stage of life — also requires planning, persistence, and a commitment to doing it right.

We've grown used to seeing midlife portrayed as a most satisfying time of life. Careers are established. Debts have been paid. Empty nesters have more time to focus on themselves and their needs. Well, if midlife is the peak, does that mean it's all downhill from there? What is it that people have in pre-retirement that they seem to lack during retirement? There seem to be a lot of answers, including purpose, goals, self-esteem, and social interaction. But these pieces don't have to be missing. Careful planning can ensure we integrate all the components of a joyful retirement.

ON BEING "OLD," "AGED," "ELDERLY"

One of the most difficult things to deal with as we progress through life is how our attitudes, and attitudes toward us, change. I vividly remember the first time my stepson and I discovered the generation gap. And I was on the wrong side. He was 19 and I was 33. So young, and yet so old! Funny, my 47-year-old husband never seems to be on the wrong side of the gap. He is firmly planted in today, and in experiencing, and in living, and in joy. (Thank heavens I've had him to reach over and grab me back whenever I threatened to wander too far onto the other side.)

As we move through the stages of our lives, we are often faced with attitudes about what's proper, appropriate, and healthy for "people our age." Sometimes we allow our children, our friends, and society as a whole to label us, and then we work very hard to live up to those labels — even when they are quite inappropriate for describing our true essence. As we get older, we may be expected to slow down, take it easy, be careful. Well, you can go muttering to your rocking chair if you wish, but I have other plans:

When I Am Old

When I am an old woman I shall wear purple
With a red hat which doesn't go, and doesn't suit me,
And I shall spend my pension on brandy and summer gloves
And satin sandals, and say we've no money for butter.
I shall sit down on the pavement when I'm tired
And gobble up samples in shops and press alarm bells
And run my stick along the public railings
And make up for the sobriety of my youth.
I shall go out in my slippers in the rain
And pick the flowers in other people's gardens
And learn to spit . . .
But maybe I ought to practice a little now?
So people who know me are not too shocked and surprised
When suddenly I am old and start to wear purple.

— Jenny Joseph

IT'S UP TO YOU

The choice is yours. You can choose to accept the stereotypes and grow old, or you can stay in tune with life and youth. You can accept the ending, or you can see retirement as a beginning of the next part of a wonderfully fulfilling life. You can choose to retire from life, or to restyle your life.

If you choose to retire from life, you don't have to do much more. If you choose to restyle, your work's just begun. Do some research on retirement and what it will be like. As much as is in your power, get healthy and stay healthy. Put your financial house in order. Attend tax, investment, and retirement-planning seminars. Check newspapers and magazine articles, and develop your own strategy for retirement. Collect Revenue Canada's and Health and Welfare Canada's tax bulletins, pamphlets, and booklets. Your objective should be to ensure you're up-to-date on what's what from both a financial and a social perspective.

That's as much philosophizing as I'm going to do. I hope you find this book helpful in outlining the things to think about, and the steps to take in planning for your retirement. I enjoyed writing it, and I hope you enjoy reading it and that you can put it to good use.

1 THE RETIREMENT QUIZ

People have a lot of misconceptions when it comes to retirement planning. Take this test and see how close your view of retirement comes to the realities you will face, and how closely you are in touch with some of the facts you'll need for retirement.

1. Rank the following ages in terms of when Canadians are most likely to retire:

    ✓ Over 65   4

    ✓ 65   3

    ✓ 60-64   1

    ✓ 55-59   2

    ✓ Younger than 55   5

2. If you purchased a straight life annuity with $100,000 of your RRSP savings, and you died the next day, how much would your spouse or estate receive from your annuity?

    ❑ $75,000   ❑ $50,000   ❑ $25,000   ☑ $0

3. When you use your spousal RRSP to buy a RRIF, if you take more than the minimum annual amount from the plan, how is your income taxed?

    ❑ The minimum is taxed as the plan-holder's income, the rest as the contributor's income.

    ❑ The minimum is taxed as the contributor's income, the rest as the plan-holder's income.

    ☑ All as the plan-holder's income.

    ❑ All as the contributor's income.

THE RETIREMENT QUIZ

4. In 1992, senior citizens collected $_____ more from social security programs than they paid in income tax.

☐ $15 billion   ☑ $25 billion   ☐ $45 billion   ☐ $65 billion

5. Inflation is a major threat to retirement security. A five percent rate of inflation over the next twenty years will reduce the purchasing power of $1 to approximately:

☑ 26¢   ☐ 38¢   ☐ 42¢   ☐ 67¢

6. While public sector employees save approximately 16 percent of their income for retirement, private sector employees save:

☑ 3%   ☑ 7%   ☐ 11%   ☐ 15%

7. You must close your RRSP by the end of the year in which you turn age:

☐ 65   ☐ 69   ☑ 71   ☐ 90

8. If you chose to take your CPP at age 62, your benefits would be reduced by:

☑ 6%   ☐ 12%   ☐ 18%   ☐ 24%

9. In 1996, about 20 percent of households are headed by people 65 and older. By 2026, that percentage will be approximately:

☐ 23%   ☑ 27%   ☐ 32%   ☐ 36%

10. Most people sell their homes when they retire.

☑ True   ☐ False

11. Older people are more risk-averse than younger people.

☑ True   ☐ False

X 12. If you do not need the income from your RRIF, but must mature your RRSP because you have reached the legal age requirement, the best way to continue deferring taxes is to take your income:

☑ monthly ☐ quarterly ☐ semi-annually ☐ annually

X 13. Working takes up a lot of time. Approximately how many hours a year will retirement free up?

☐ 1,000 ☐ 1,500 ☐ 2,000 ☑ 2,500

14. The amount you earn on your retirement assets will play a significant part in how long those assets will last. Between 1949 and 1993, Canada Savings Bonds had an average return of:

☐ 5.6% ☐ 8.3% ☑ 9.7% ☐ 10.8%

15. Between 1949 and 1993, Canadian stocks had an average return of:

☑ 8.3% ☐ 9.7% ☐ 10.8% ☐ 12.6%

16. What percentage of people retired because they had reached the mandatory age?

☐ 14% ☐ 20% ☑ 23% ☐ 31%

17. What is the number-one reason given for retirement?

☐ Mandatory   ☐ Family   ☐ Spouse   ☑ Health
   age   reasons   retired   reasons

X 18. In 1994, what percentage of retired women lived on an income of less than $15,000 per year?

☐ 23% ☑ 37% ☐ 54% ☐ 62%

THE ANSWERS

1. Over 65 – 4; 65 – 3; 60-64 – 1; 55-59 – 2; Younger than 55 – 5
2. $0
3. The minimum is taxed as the plan-holder's income, the rest as the contributor's income.
4. $45 billion[1]
5. 38¢
6. 7%[2]
7. 69
8. 18%
9. 32%[3]
10. False. Most retired people remain in their homes for as long as they can.[4]
11. False. Older people are usually more realistic in their decision-making, taking only necessary risks, not foolish ones.[5]
12. Annually
13. 2,000
14. 8.3%
15. 10.8%
16. 14%
17. Health reasons
18. 62%

[1] Troubled Tomorrows, The Report of the Canadian Institute of Actuaries' Task Force on Retirement Savings
[2] Ibid.
[3] Roger Suave, *Canadian People Patterns*, Prairie Books
[4] James Lynch and Gail Riddell, *Retirement Education: A Multi-Group Discussion Approach*
[5] Ibid.

2 TO RETIRE OR NOT TO RETIRE . . .

Retirement can be either the best time of your life, or the most disappointing. Many are the stories told of people who could hardly wait to retire. When they finally reached this milepost, they couldn't figure out what to do next. As Laurence Peter said, "Retirement is the time when you never do all the things you intended to do when you'd have the time."

Attitudes toward retirement are changing. Canada is experiencing a boom in people 65 and older. Approximately one in 10 Canadians is now in this group, and it is estimated that by the year 2031 the number will be one in four. As the baby boom generation — those born between 1946 and 1966 — grows older, we will likely see significant changes in the way society defines concepts such as "retirement" and "seniors." The boomers will do for the over-65 age group exactly what they've done all along as they've moved through the other age groups: redefine, remake, and popularize it. These boomers know that retirement isn't the end of a life. It's the beginning of a new, more carefree, and personally focused phase of their lives.

Whether you are approaching retirement chomping at the bit, or dreading the prospect of having nothing to do, a little time spent planning will help you ease into retirement with realistic expectations. Don't wait until your retirement date arrives to make all the decisions that must be made. Start early, plan carefully, and set objectives that are attainable. And the earlier you start, the more time you'll have to overcome any previously unforeseen obstacles that arise.

WHEN TO RETIRE

To retire or not to retire? For many years this question was easily answered. You retire when you're 65, right? Not necessarily. Pensions have become more flexible. Changes in government policies and a greater commitment to personal retirement savings mean we have more choices about retirement. We can retire early — some as early as 50. We can continue working in our current jobs until we are 70 or more. Or we can retire and start a new career. It is estimated that the projected decline in the labour market will keep older people in the workforce far longer than ever before. And many of these people will be self-employed, mixing retirement and employment to meet their individual needs.

We also have much more choice in terms of the lifestyle we choose for retirement. Retiring couples are trading in their rocking chairs for airline seats, bicycles, and hot-air balloons. Free of children and other external responsibilities, retirees can do what they want, when they want.

Retirees will also be the swinging singles of the future. It is expected that the number of single, widowed, and divorced people will surge — making up more than 25 percent of all households — and more than two-thirds of those singles will be over 65. This has significant implications for the way society will restructure itself. Older single people will not only have to be independent financially, they will also have to take responsibility for building friendships to fulfill their needs for social interaction and intimacy.

ATTITUDES TOWARD RETIREMENT

It isn't all that odd that the magic age of 65 has traditionally been seen as the age at which people will move into the next phase of their lives. Government and most private pension plans use 65 as their normal retirement age. However, a growing number of Canadians are beginning to look at the age at which they retire with slightly different eyes. Mandatory retirement has been hotly debated. Many people consider employment after they've reached 65 an economic necessity. Other trends such as early retirement, gradual retirement, economic cutbacks, and multiple careers are challenging the way many people consider when they will retire and, indeed, what retirement itself will be like.

The General Social Survey (GSS) conducted by Statistics Canada in 1994 showed that among the currently employed, 45 percent plan to retire before 65. Of the remaining, 14 percent plan to retire at 65, and two percent want to retire after age 65. Eight percent don't intend to retire at all and the rest don't know when they'll retire.

Since 1989, there has been a greater diversity of retirement age. While 16 percent of people retired at age 65 in 1989, by 1994 that number dropped to only 10 percent. Approximately 67 percent of people retired before the age of 65. That's up from 64 percent in the 1989 survey. This further indicates a trend to earlier retirement.

Age at Retirement	Percentage of Respondents	
	1989	1994
65+	20	23
65	16	10
60-64	29	32
55-59	19	21
≤54	16	14

Many people are being faced with forced early retirement because of difficult economic conditions. Between 1990 and 1994, the number of people retiring while unemployed rose by 30 percent over the 1985-to-1989 figures. In 1994, the average age for men citing this reason was 62.1 years, and for women 59.6 years.

Reason for Retirement	Percentage of Respondents
Reached mandatory age	14
Early retirement	7
Health	24
Unemployment	10
Choice	23
Spouse retired	3
Family reasons	6
Person feels old enough	10
Other	3

The GSS provides a rather broad-brushed picture of the reasons for retirement. However, it clearly indicates that the likelihood of early retirement is highest for those people receiving employer-sponsored pension benefits.

Since 1970, the availability of early retirement with and without a reduction in benefits has increased. For example, the percentage of registered pension plan (RPP) members with an option of early retirement on a reduced pension grew from 87 percent of the 2.8 million members in 1970 to 98 percent of the 5 million members in 1989.

FOCUSING ON WOMEN

Canadian women, in particular, are at risk for financially insecure retirements. In general, women retire earlier than men. In 1994, the average retirement age for women was 58.5 years, compared with 61.4 for men. Women also live longer than men — by between six and seven years. That means women are facing a longer life living on a fixed income. As well, women typically have a smaller retirement savings pool on which to draw during retirement.

A number of factors contribute to the situation in which Canadian women are finding themselves in retirement. Traditionally, it is women who take time from their work lives to raise families and care for loved ones. In fact, while 13 percent of women retire for family reasons (i.e., child care and rearing or caring for a sick spouse or relative), no men choose to retire for this reason. Similarly, while seven percent of women retire when their husbands retire, men do not leave the workforce simply because their wives do.

Historically, elderly women have been economically disadvantaged. In 1994, 62 percent of retired women were living on an income of less than $15,000 while 30 percent lived on less than $10,000 (compared to 34 percent and 13 percent respectively for men.) These women rely heavily on government support. According to Statistics Canada, of those women who started their careers at the age of 25 in 1991, 82 percent will require financial assistance during retirement, while an additional 11 percent will be working whether they want to or not. In fact, only two percent of women will enjoy a lifestyle close to the one they enjoyed while working.

Over time, this picture will improve somewhat, primarily due to changes in pension legislation and a more aggressive approach to the accumulation of personal assets. Women's increased participation in the labour market has also resulted in their increased participation in government- and employer-sponsored pension plans, as well as in private registered plans (RRSPs). In 1978, female RRSP contributors were uncommon — only six percent of all women who filed a tax return had taken advantage of the tax deferral and retirement savings benefits offered by an RRSP. By 1989, participation by women had increased to 21 percent. Between 1991 and 1993, 35 percent of eligible women made RRSP contributions. It is expected that as more women enter the job market, as pay equity and female promotion programs are strengthened, and as men and women get rid of outdated stereotypes, the female-to-male wage disadvantage will narrow.

Changes in divorce laws have also had a positive impact on women's financial positions. Since January 1987, the sharing of government pension benefits has been mandatory in the case of separation or divorce. As more women have become aware of this option, the number who have applied for a credit from the split of government pension due to marriage breakdown has risen. To qualify for the splitting of credits, the ex-spouses must have lived together for at least 36 consecutive months, and the application must be made within three years of the divorce becoming final.

Despite the fact that the picture has improved for women, they still currently receive substantially less than men in retirement income. While 48 percent of men retired from managerial and professional employment received an income of $30,000 a year or more, only 17 percent of women in this category managed this high an income. Sixty-one percent had an income of less than $20,000 (compared with 22 percent of men). In the clerical, sales, and services category, only 20 percent of women retired with an income of more than $20,000 (compared with 40 percent of men).

For women retiring in the future, the onus is on them to take personal responsibility for how well they will live during retirement. We all must take the time to educate ourselves: read everything in sight, attend seminars, ask for help. We also have to take control of our finances, develop an action plan, and follow through to meet our objectives. It's not rocket science. It's good, sound financial planning. And it's about time!

ARE YOU READY TO RETIRE?

With retirement comes significant change, and negative reactions to retirement are not uncommon. This is particularly true for people who are forced to retire earlier than anticipated because of either health or economic circumstances.

The first significant change you'll likely face is the economic impact of the end of the paycheque. You may feel uneasy as you wonder how much of that paycheque will be replaced by income from pensions, investments, and savings. Will you be able to maintain your lifestyle and do all the things you've dreamed of? There are many things you can do to plan and put your mind at rest for the financial impact of retirement, and these are covered in detail in chapter 3.

The second significant change is the psychological impact of leaving work. This will differ from person to person, depending on how much the job has functioned as a source of identity, provided social contacts, and served to structure time. The more dependent you have been on your work for each of these, the more careful you must be about planning how to cope with the impact of this ending.

WHO AM I?

Many of us define ourselves, or at least part of our identity, by the work we do. How often have you been asked (or asked of someone else), "What do you do?" If your work functions as a source of status and self-esteem for you, retirement may mean a loss of identity and a feeling of less personal worth. If you put a great deal of emphasis on what you do for a living, you must take time to determine if it is only your work by which you define yourself, or if there are other aspects of your life that contribute to your status, identity, and self-esteem.

HELLO? HELLO? ARE YOU THERE?

The amount you depend on your work for social contact will also have a significant impact on how you deal with retirement. Often when people leave work, they have difficulty maintaining their work-based relationships. This means that part of your planning for retirement should focus on building a network of relationships that are not dependent on your work environment. As well, as you move into retirement, you'll need to find ways of replacing the friendships that may disappear. You can do this by joining organizations, participating in activities in which you already have interests, and exploring new areas. Perhaps there is an area of study or a hobby you've always been interested in; now you have time to explore it further. Meeting people with a similar interest can be a good basis for forming new friendships.

PUTTING TIME ON YOUR SIDE

Before you actually retire, the thought of having unlimited time to do just what you want may seem like Utopia. However, unless your time is structured and includes obligations requiring effort on your part, often all that time becomes both boring and frustrating.

Work provides a structure for the use of time. Many of us are conditioned to working full days, usually against time pressures. Some people find it difficult to use their time meaningfully once the formal structure disappears. It is not enough to fill your time by just keeping busy. You need to use your time in ways that will be personally satisfying. Activities you enjoyed and found satisfying prior to retirement will likely continue to be satisfying, so look for ways to maintain or even expand these. If you have skills from your work life that can be transferred to other activities, you may want to investigate working part-time, consulting, or volunteering.

Unfortunately, until we do an analysis of our time, most of us have no idea how much time we actually spend on the various activities we do. Here's an exercise you may wish to try to help you figure out just how you spend your time.

Make two copies of the diagram on the following page. Each column represents one day of the week and each diamond represents one hour of the day. On the first diagram, use crayons or markers to colour in the appropriate number of squares for each day as you answer the following questions.

MY TIME NOW

Blue   How many hours do you spend in work-related activities? If you bring home work, or spend time commuting, include that time.

Red   How many hours do you spend on activities such as showering, eating, exercising, etc.?

Yellow   How many hours do you spend sleeping?

Purple   How many hours do you spend attending to your household duties such as housekeeping, cooking, shopping, laundry, gardening, snow shovelling, etc. If you spend

11

MON	TUES	WED	THURS	FRI	SAT	SUN

time on occasional jobs such as paying bills or doing home repairs, include those.

Green   How much time do you spend in casual socializing with your family and friends?

Orange   How much time do you spend in leisure activities such as sports, hobbies, and activities involving others?

Black   How much time do you spend in solitary activities such as reading, watching television, listening to music, hobbies you do by yourself?

Brown   How much time do you spend in formal socializing (as a member of a club, organization, volunteer group, etc.)?

Now, fill in the second diagram you copied with how you would like your time to look during retirement. Keep in mind that with reduced time spent on family maintenance, work, professional associations, and other pre-retirement activities, increased time will need to be allocated to other activities.

Also, keep in mind that:

- Many of your current interests will be important to you when you retire. If you are an avid gardener now, you will likely want to continue gardening. A community centre that provides greenhouse facilities for the winter may be of interest. Alternatively, you may want to join a garden club or build a solarium on your home before you retire so that when you move into retirement a base has already been laid.

- Your partner will have something to say about the way you both spend your time. Work together so that no conflicts arise later. While the two of you should do this exercise individually, you must also come together and share your ideas so that you have mutually agreeable expectations.

- You may end up spending part of your retirement alone. If you're a woman, this is of particular importance since women tend to live longer than men. Make sure you know your financial position. Also, make sure you develop an emotional safety net of family, friends, and activities so that you do not feel alone and abandoned.

- Your family may have strong opinions about what you should or should not do with your retirement. For example, you may want to spend time in a warm place, while your children want you to be readily available to them. You won't have to live your life for them (those days are gone), but you should try to be sensitive to their feelings. They may need reassurance about your financial, emotional, and health circumstances. They will also be facing their own demons as your retirement brings them face-to-face with the fact that they are also aging.

ON BECOMING INVOLVED

The trick to maintaining your self-esteem, status, and identity during retirement is to become really involved in whatever it is you are doing. Whether expanding current activities or exploring new alternatives, focus on things from which you gain real satisfaction and a sense of purpose. After all, retirement is a time for doing what you *want* to do. So what do you *want* to do?

- Take the trip you've been dreaming of?
- Help others, through volunteer work?
- Study a subject you've been interested in?
- Expand an activity that work didn't allow much time for?

Start by listing all the things you enjoy and the things you're particularly good at. Choose to expand or get involved in the things you feel you will gain the most satisfaction from. The better you are at what it is you are doing, the more likely you are to enjoy it.

VARIETY IS THE SPICE OF LIFE

As we move through the earlier stages of our lives, work and family responsibilities force us into the world to experience. Whether we are involved in our children's sports, hobbies, and schooling, or in associations and professional groups associated with our careers, we are constantly being exposed to new people. In retirement, with families grown and careers left behind, we have to find new reasons for getting out and about. It is very easy just to stay home — day in and day out. Nothing contributes more to boredom and lethargy.

It is important that you not wait until retirement to plan how you will use your retirement time. The patterns of activity you establish in midlife will likely continue into retirement. If you have traditionally been a joiner, enjoyed cultural activities, and looked outside yourself for stimulation, you will most likely continue in this vein. However, if you have had a tendency to be a loner, to spend much of your time reading, watching television, or on other me-focused activities, you will find yourself spending more time alone simply because you have more time. Without the external motivations of children and work to force you out, you may become less interactive. And, as you become less interactive, it will seem easier to avoid involvement. Take charge, chart your own course, and set routines with which you are comfortable. Your objective should be to interact — meet people, experience new activities, share ideas, and keep in touch with the world around you.

Consider, too, that it may take time for you to find what you like to do most with all the time you have on your hands. Experience! If it turns out you don't like a particular activity, you can always stop. Experiment! Try new hobbies, become a volunteer, go on group outings. Never say no to an opportunity to try something new, or see something you've never seen before. Enjoy! That's the whole purpose of retirement . . . remember?

CHOOSING A RETIREMENT DATE

With boomers choosing to retire while they are still young — in their mid to late fifties and early sixties — there are a number of issues that have to be carefully considered.

First, early retirement means that your retirement savings must last longer. Second, early retirement means you'll have less time to accumulate the money needed to support your retirement dreams. And since many pension plans' benefits are based on your years of service and earnings, early retirement can significantly reduce your pension. These aspects can significantly change how you view your retirement, and the date you pick. Realistically evaluate whether your assets will be sufficient to provide the income you'll need during the additional years of retirement. Think about how much your spouse will need to live on his or her own.

If you are an independent business-person, you'll also have to think about what you will do with your business. For the professional, the sale of a practice will require an evaluation and, perhaps, some financial advice. For a business manager who plans to pass on the business, management continuity will be important. Not only do you have to think about your own retirement plans, but how those plans will affect all those people you work with.

If both you and your spouse work outside the home, you'll have to decide whether you will retire together or stagger your retirements. Take into account where you are in your careers, your commitment and interest in the work you are doing, and your expectations for retirement. Think about each of your retirement savings portfolios and how you will allocate your funds when creating a retirement income. Finally, think about spending all that time together.

Retirement frees up approximately 2,000 hours a year. Well, when was the last time you spent 2,000 hours with your spouse? Are you ready for that yet? Staggering your entry, with one starting a year or two before the other, will help to ease you both comfortably into a mutually satisfying retirement. The first to retire can ease the second into the retirement stream by providing valuable advice about what to expect and how to cope. The last to retire can provide a financial safety net for the first to investigate options for an active and productive retirement. Together you can move into retirement smoothly and harmoniously.

RESTYLING YOUR LIFE

While retirement is a good time for trying new lifestyles, continuity is important, and you should approach significant lifestyle changes cautiously. Don't rush into radical moves such as changing your housing, moving to a new location, or starting a new (unfamiliar) business. Remember, you need time to adapt. Be realistic about what you can and cannot handle both short- and long-term. Plan carefully and practise before you make major changes. For example, if you plan to relocate to a new community, try renting there for about six months before you make a final decision to buy.

RETIREMENT CONSIDERATIONS

Where do you plan to live? In the same house or apartment, or are you planning to sell and move to a smaller home? The majority of most people's financial assets are tied up in their homes. Folks figure that when they retire, they'll sell, buy a smaller place, and have lots of money left over.

But do you really want to move . . . away from your family . . . away from your neighbours . . . away from everything that's familiar? Most people don't, despite their well-laid plans.

For some people the decision to move is easy. Perhaps they're attracted by warmer climes. Or maybe the house is just too big or inappropriate for their needs (see pages 18-20). For some the lure of a small town or being part of a retirement community is very attractive.

Many lower-cost housing alternatives exist that you may wish to look into. Subsidized dwellings are not limited to public housing; non-profit housing and cooperative housing developments also offer alternatives geared to a retiree's income. Canada Mortgage & Housing Corporation (CMHC) has information that may help you decide how you want to live in retirement. Contact your local CMHC office for copies of *Housing Choices for Older Canadians* and start learning about your alternatives. You can also get information on subsidized housing from non-profit and cooperative housing agencies.

If you decide your present home isn't suitable for retirement, you'll have to decide whether you will move within your community, divide your time between two communities (perhaps your cottage in the summer and autumn, and a warm climate in the winter and spring), or move to a whole new area. Keep in mind that there are special considerations that must be given to moving to a whole new community and to spending all or part of your time in another country. Where you'll live must be carefully considered not only in terms of how much money you'll need during retirement, but also in terms of what you want to do during retirement.

SO, ARE YOU REALLY READY TO RETIRE?

In trying to determine if you are ready to retire, consider the following questions:

1. Are you in a financial position to maintain your lifestyle and achieve what you desire for your retirement? (See chapter 3 for a detailed analysis of this aspect.)

2. How important is your work to you? Does your work provide status and identity? Are you mentally ready to change from a work lifestyle to a retirement lifestyle?

3. Do you depend on your work environment for the majority of your social contacts? How will you replace these in retirement?

4. Do you need something external to structure your time?

5. What types of interests do you have outside of work? Are these interests involving and fulfilling? Can you expand the time you spend in these interests? Do your plans account for your spouse's desires?

6. How do you spend your leisure time? Do you become restless on weekends or during holidays? Will you be able to use your time in a way that will make retirement enjoyable?

7. Is your current home appropriate for retirement? Do you plan to stay in your community? If you plan to move, are you familiar with the new community?

IS YOUR CURRENT HOME APPROPRIATE FOR YOUR RETIREMENT?

1. Will your mortgage be paid when you retire? Will there be any debts remaining on your home?

2. Does the house need any work such as painting, new rugs, new roof, or furnace?

3. How high will your maintenance expenses be? What about your taxes? Will your income be sufficient for you to live *comfortably* in the home?

4. Have your space needs changed significantly? Can part of the home be used to provide a rental income? Do you want to maintain a larger home so you have the space to accommodate visiting relatives?

5. Do you feel safe and secure in the home? Are there features you may find difficult in the future (e.g., too many stairs, inadequate lighting, slippery floors, large lawn, long driveway, etc.)? Can features be added to increase your sense of safety and security (e.g., a grab bar in the shower)?

6. Will your home hold its value over time? Do neighbours maintain their homes?

7. Is your home set up with room for your hobbies and other activities?

8. What features of your home are you planning to change prior to retirement? Have you budgeted to cover the costs?

9. Do you have the energy to maintain your home? What will it cost to hire help (snow removal, grass cutting, housekeeping, etc.)?

10. Are there health or climate considerations you should weigh?

11. How does the rest of your family feel about your home?

12. How much more income would you have if you sold your house, eliminated your maintenance/tax costs, and rented?

Approximate value of home	$ _____
Less sales-related costs	$ _____
Balance to invest	$ _____
Return expected at ____%	$ _____
Tax payable on return	$ _____
Net return	$ _____
Net return	$ _____
Plus savings on maintenance*	$ _____
Less estimated cost of rental†	$ _____
Balance	$ _____

* When you sell your home, you'll likely eliminate many of your expenses such as property tax, snow removal, gardening, house maintenance, heating, and hydro. Remember, unless your rent includes these costs, you'll still have to make provisions for some utility costs and, of course, things like cable.

† Make sure you choose a comparable home, one you'll be happy to live in. Check the newspaper for the prices of rentals in areas in which you'd feel comfortable living. Investigate subsidized-housing alternatives. Don't underestimate your space requirements. Often people who move from houses to apartments feel "squeezed." Heed the words of a wise man: "Let there be space between your togetherness."

13. How close is your home to public transportation? How close are you to stores? Do those stores deliver?

14. How many of your interests and activities take place close to your home? How close do you live to other family members? How close are you (emotionally) to your neighbours?

15. Is home-sharing an alternative for you? How much income could you generate? Would sharing provide you with help around the house?

16. Could you renovate your home into two living units and rent out one to supplement your income?

WHAT WILL YOUR LIFESTYLE BE LIKE WHEN YOU RETIRE?

1. Where will you live?

2. How will your housing needs change?

3. How much of your time will you need to spend in household duties (grocery shopping, laundry, etc.)? How much time will you spend with family? On your hobbies and interests? In community activities?

4. What interests will you pursue now that you have more time?

5. How will you maintain contacts with workplace friends? How will you make new friends? Will you entertain often? Formally or informally?

6. What would you like to change about your lifestyle as you move into retirement?

7. What new challenges are you going to take on when you retire?

8. Who will you share activities with during retirement?

9. What type of sports and recreational facilities are available to you in retirement? Which activities most interest you?

10. If you plan to move closer to your children, how will that affect the rest of your retirement activities? Your friendships?

SETTING YOUR FINANCIAL GOALS

If you want your retirement to go just so, you need to set some specific financial goals toward which you will consistently work. The key is to ensure your goals are both reasonable and achievable. If you haven't given much thought to what you want to achieve or if your goals are vague, now is the time to make them concrete.

Perhaps you want to accumulate a specific amount of money, eliminate your mortgage and credit card debt, or pay off a new car before you retire. Weighing each of your goals against the others will help you to see which are the most important (see page 43).

Whenever you set a goal, write it down and make it as specific as possible. It's not enough to establish broad goals without specific details. For example, instead of a general statement such as "I want to establish an emergency fund," in setting a goal, you would say, "I want to have an emergency fund of $10,000 established by January 15, 19__." With written goals and specific target dates, you can measure how your financial plan is shaping up each year.

While the goals you set will be specific to your personal needs and circumstances, make sure you look at your total financial picture and bring everything into balance. The five main components of a sound financial plan include:
1. Money management
2. Risk management
3. Retirement planning
4. Investment strategies/tax planning
5. Estate planning.

To ensure a balanced and well-rounded financial plan for retirement, you should have goals set within each of these five areas.

Money Management

Begin by eliminating your consumer debt, such as credit card balances and loans. Often people pay only the minimum required without realizing how much interest costs work against their overall plan. If your monthly credit card balance is on the high end of the average ($1,200 to $2,400), and your card charges the typical 17 percent, you're paying $400 a year in interest. If you have several cards with high balances, consider a consolidation loan to reduce your interest costs. If your card charges a high rate of interest, transfer your balance to lower-cost card. If you have only a small amount to work off, put your cards away until the debt is cleared. Once you're debt free, by all means take advantage of the convenience credit cards offer, but keep tight control of them. When you pay off your balance in full every month, you'll receive an interest-free loan from the credit card company for the period between your purchase and your credit card due date. That's smart money management!

Risk Management

Next you have to prepare for the risks of everyday life. The ones we seem to deal with quite easily are property insurance, car insurance, contents insurance. Think about an emergency fund to protect you and your family against unexpected situations — things like forced early retirement or health care costs or property losses that won't be covered by insurance. Also, check your insurance coverage to make sure you have enough disability, health, life, property, and casualty insurance.

Your objective is to be able to meet all your financial needs without straining your resources. If you have dependants — a dependent spouse, children, grandchildren, or elderly parents — make sure they are taken care of.

Retirement Planning

Retirement planning shouldn't end at retirement. After all, you'll likely spend as long in retirement as you did working. And since retirement means different things to different people, and has its own series of stages, you need to keep planning for the next stage.

You may, for example, begin by semi-retiring. Stage One would include working part-time, starting a new business, or working as a consultant.

In Stage Two of your retirement, you may plan to stop working completely while you remain very active in other areas. Your active retirement might include extensive travel, activities such as golfing, skiing, or cycling, or active volunteering.

Stage Three would be your less active years — the years when you plan to remain in your home, with or without help from others.

Stage Four may be the years when you choose to move to a retirement home that provides you with the help you need in managing day-to-day activities along with specialized medical attention.

Investment Strategies/Tax Planning

Just as you had to manage your investments carefully during your working years, so too will you have to manage your investments carefully during your retirement years. Minimizing your tax will be even more important as you strive to live on a fixed income. As investments mature and economic conditions change, you will have to make important decisions about new investments and reinvestments. You need to stay in tune with the financial world, or you'll need a guide who can provide you with the information to make informed decisions. Some people are willing to accept help from their children. Others feel more comfortable with an impartial financial adviser. Whichever you prefer, just make sure you've established the relationships you need, and the objectives for your retirement portfolio, well ahead of time.

Estate Planning

Despite the fact that almost everyone should have a will and a power of attorney, many people don't. Some think their wishes will be carried out by a family member or that they do not have enough money to justify the cost of making a will. Others avoid making a will because their personal circumstances — marriages, divorces, and accumulated children and stepchildren — just seem too complex to unravel. However, if you die without a will, trying to figure out who gets what, and when, can be a mess. And your estate may end up paying more in fees and taxes than it should, leaving less for your loved ones.

MONITORING YOUR RETIREMENT PLAN

Don't forget to do a semi-annual review of your retirement goals to check your progress. Having taken control, you'll have a better understanding of your financial situation and will be able to achieve the things you want. Of course, a sound retirement plan isn't built overnight. It takes time, a strong commitment, and, perhaps, a retirement counsellor. Most of all, it takes a belief in yourself and in your own ability to make your retirement all you want it to be.

3 RETIREMENT-INCOME PLANNING

What have you planned for retirement? Golf? Warm winters? Cycling through Europe? Retirement means you finally have the freedom to live your life exactly as you wish. No more children. No more employers. No more time constraints. Now you can do all the things you've always dreamed of. However, taking maximum advantage of all the choices retirement offers requires some planning. By developing new skills as a rehearsal for retirement, you can set the stage for a more orderly transition. And, if you happen to be forced into retirement before you're ready, you'll be better able to deal effectively with your change in circumstances.

That planning can be broken into three time frames:

- before retirement — when there's still time to accumulate and organize assets, and plan the transition to the next phase in your life

- the point of retirement — where decisions must be made regarding a retirement income and your choice of lifestyle

- after retirement — ongoing decisions must be made to deal with changes in personal, economic, and social circumstances.

In this chapter, we will look at the steps you should take before you retire and the financial implications of retirement-income planning. Most people recognize the need to plan financially for their retirements. They know they'll need a fair amount of money; they're not sure how much they'll need or how much to save. Some people find that after taxes and living expenses there's little or nothing left. Others aren't sure what to invest their retirement savings in. Still others don't even want to think about it because the whole idea of retirement-income planning is intimidating.

Retirement-income planning isn't as complicated as it may first appear. In essence, you need to know where you are now and where you want to be at retirement. Then you have to design a savings and investment strategy to get you there.

First, let's begin by looking at the sources of income that are available for supporting your retirement dreams.

GOVERNMENT PENSIONS

WHO GETS OAS?

In 1952 Canada introduced the Old Age Security (OAS) system to provide income security universally across Canada. Back then, everyone over 70 was entitled to $40 a month.

The OAS system consists of:

- OAS pension
- the Guaranteed Income Supplement (GIS)
- the Spouse's Allowance (SA).

OAS pension is a basic benefit paid monthly to all Canadians who are 65 or older and meet the Canadian residency requirements. In 1996 the maximum OAS pension paid was approximately $4,650.

Until July 1, 1977, the eligibility period was 40 years' residence in Canada after the age of 18. Alternatively, if you had 10 years' legal residence in Canada immediately before the application, you could claim full OAS benefits.

New rules introduced in 1977 changed the way OAS benefits are calculated. Now, people earn 2.5 percent of the OAS benefit for each year of residence in Canada after age 18. However, unless Canada has a social security agreement with the person's previous country, at least 10 years' residence in Canada is needed before the minimum pension (one-quarter of the full OAS) is allowed. People who became residents of Canada before July 1, 1977, can choose to qualify under either set of rules, but the older rules will likely be more beneficial.

If you plan to leave Canada after you retire, there's a "20-year rule" that stipulates you must have lived in Canada for at least 20 years after age 18 before you can receive your benefits outside of Canada indefinitely. If you don't qualify under this 20-year rule, you'll receive OAS benefits for the month you leave and for six months afterward. Benefits will be suspended at that point, and you'll have to reapply and requalify if you return to Canada.

25

The Guaranteed Income Supplement is a monthly benefit paid to people who get an OAS pension but have little or no other income. GIS benefits are limited by an income threshold that is adjusted quarterly according to the increase in the consumer price index. In 1996 the maximum GIS annual benefit paid to an individual was $5,529.48, and recipients had to have an income of $11,063.90 or less to qualify; more than three million Canadians — almost half of all pensioners — qualified. GIS benefits are not taxable and you must apply for benefits every year.

The Spouse's Allowance is provided to spouses (age 60-64) of people receiving OAS pension benefits whose family income does not exceed a certain limit. In 1996 the maximum annual SA benefit paid was $8,254.56, and recipients had to have an income of $20,687.99 or less to qualify.

To find out how to qualify for OAS and to get the details of the amounts currently being paid under the OAS system, contact Human Resources Development Canada. You can find the number in the blue pages of your telephone directory.

● ●

OAS benefits aren't automatic; you have to apply for them. You'd be wise to send in your application about six months before your 65th birthday to ensure you begin receiving benefits on time. Once you are approved for OAS benefits, you will receive a form that will be used to determine if you qualify for the GIS.

● ●

WHAT IS THE OAS CLAWBACK?

In 1989, the federal government announced that anyone with retirement income above $50,000 a year must repay part or all of their Old Age Security (OAS). This limit is partially indexed for inflation with the first three percent of any increase in the consumer price index excluded. (In 1996, the threshold was $53,215 per person and total OAS was clawed back when an individual's income exceeded $80,000.) This limit is applicable to individuals; currently there is no family-income provision. So, if your income exceeds the threshold, you'll be assessed a tax on any income above the threshold, at a rate of 15 percent, up to the total of all the OAS you've received. This means that for every $100 in income you receive above the threshold amount, you have to pay back $15 of your OAS benefits.

> Anthony Preston received OAS benefits of $4,500. His net income was $60,000. Since his income exceeded the allowable threshold of $53,000 by $7,000, the difference was clawed back at a rate of 15 percent. That means he had to repay $1,050 in OAS benefits. Anthony's brother, Stephen, had an income of $95,000. All of Stephen's OAS benefits were clawed back.

The most effective way to beat the clawback is to split your income as evenly as possible between yourself and your spouse. This way, you and your spouse could have a joint income of over $100,000 and not be affected by the clawback. See chapter 5 for more information on income splitting.

• •

One way to reduce the impact of the OAS clawback is to delay receiving your CPP/QPP benefits until you absolutely need them to meet your expenses.

• •

If you *are* subject to the OAS clawback, by managing your income you can still claim at least some benefits. By arranging to have a particularly high income in one year and a lower income the following year, you'll be able to benefit from OAS at least every other year.

> Cora Lightfoot retired three years ago. What with the spousal benefit on her deceased husband's pension plan, her own company pension, and the income she was taking from her Registered Retirement Income Fund (RRIF), Cora was losing quite a bit of her OAS benefit to the clawback. So Cora restructured her income to maximize her OAS entitlement.

In December 1994 she made a withdrawal from her RRIF equal to most of the income (above the minimum payout requirement) she would need in 1995. Since she took the funds in 1994, they were taxable in 1994. In 1995 Cora took only the minimum amount required by law from her RRIF, reducing her overall income that year by almost $12,000. That meant that for 1995 she fell below the income threshold and could collect all her OAS benefits.

By making a larger than normal withdrawal from her RRIF in one year, and a smaller withdrawal the next, Cora managed her income to take advantage of OAS at least every other year.

WHO GETS CPP/QPP?

The employment-related Canada Pension Plan (CPP) and Quebec Pension Plan (QPP) were introduced in 1966. These are contributory social insurance plans for which benefits are based on earnings; they pay a pension based on the number of years of contribution and pensionable earnings. A contributor must be a salaried or self-employed worker, age 18 to 70, and have annual earnings exceeding a minimum threshold. This minimum is adjusted each year.

Before 1984, people had to wait until they turned 65 to be eligible to receive CPP/QPP benefits. In 1984 (QPP) and 1987 (CPP), people who had "wholly or substantially ceased pensionable employment" were permitted access to these benefits as early as age 60. You are considered to have substantially ceased pensionable employment if your annual earnings from employment or self-employment do not exceed the maximum retirement pension payable at age 65 for the year the pension is claimed. CPP/QPP benefits are *reduced* .5 percent per month, or 6 percent per year for every year that the early retirement precedes a recipient's 65th birthday. On the flip side, if you delay taking benefits until after you've turned 65 (the latest you can wait is till age 70), your benefits would be *increased* by .5 percent per month.

SHOULD I TAKE CPP EARLY OR SHOULD I WAIT?

WHAT CPP PAYS

Maximum monthly CPP benefits in 1996

Age When Claims Begins	Payment
60	$509
65	727
70	945

If you take CPP early (before age 65) you'll receive a reduced amount for more years. If you take your CPP benefits later, you'll receive more per month, but for fewer years overall. The answer, obviously, is whichever earns you more over the long run. But that takes a little bit of future-gazing and a really good guess about how long you'll live. It also depends on whether you intend to spend the money or invest it for the future.

Generally, you'll benefit from taking your CPP/QPP early if you're single, plan to spend the money, and are unlikely to live past 77. If you're married but your spouse won't receive the survivor benefits because she'll already receive the maximum CPP (or she'll predecease you), you'll also likely be better off drawing your CPP early. Of course, if you need the money immediately to meet your day-to-day living expenses, then go ahead and take your benefits early.

Consider waiting to take your CPP/QPP benefits if your surviving spouse will need the survivor benefits from your plan to meet his needs. Also, if you expect to live a long, long time, or are concerned about the impact inflation will have on your income, waiting until age 65 or even 70 may be better for you.

• •

If you plan to retire early, but intend to wait before claiming your CPP benefits, call and find out what the impact will be on your payments. Several years of no contributions before you've reached 65 may reduce the amount of pension to which you're entitled.

• •

29

WHAT HAPPENS TO MY CPP BENEFITS WHEN I DIE?

In the event of your death, a lump-sum death benefit is paid to your estate. If your surviving spouse is 35 or older, he or she will receive a CPP survivor's pension. If your spouse is younger than 35 but maintains your dependants, he or she is also eligible for survivor benefits.

Survivor benefits continue even after remarriage, so if your benefits are cut off after you remarry, apply to have them reinstated.

Children of a CPP contributor who has died or begun to receive CPP disability benefits are entitled to flat-rate benefits that continue until age 18, or until age 25 if attending school full-time. If a child has lost the earning power of both CPP-contributing parents through disability or death, that child can claim two benefits.

Check with your local office of the CPP or QPP for details. You can find their numbers in the blue pages of your telephone directory. Ask for an up-to-date CPP/QPP Contributor Statement and, if you're only a few years away from retirement, ask for a statement each year so you can update your files.

> **As with OAS benefits, CPP benefits aren't automatic. You have to apply. If you forget to apply, or delay and change your mind, your benefits will now be paid retroactively for up to one year. To ensure you're covered, you should probably apply about six months before you intend to start receiving benefits.**

CPP benefits are not assignable; they can only be paid to you. Benefits can be automatically deposited to your bank account. If you expect to be out of the country for a period of time, or if you simply want to save yourself a trip to the bank, arrange for the amount to be automatically deposited to your account. You'll be particularly thankful you did the next time the post office decides to strike.

WHY WOULD I WANT TO SPLIT CPP BENEFITS?

Now, suppose you find that your projected retirement income is considerably higher than your spouse's. You'll probably end up paying more tax than necessary, right? Right! However, there may be a way to even out your income. Splitting your CPP benefits means your spouse will receive more income while you receive less. This can reduce or even eliminate the OAS clawback. It may also put each of you in a lower tax bracket so you'll lower your total family tax bill. Unfortunately, QPP benefits cannot be split.

> When Frank Foltrana worked out his likely retirement income, he knew he had a problem. He was projecting a retirement income of $45,000 with about $7,000 coming from CPP. Meanwhile, since his wife, Nancy, had left the workplace to raise a family, she would receive only about $1,500 a year from CPP. Because the Foltranas had been married for 40 years — longer than Frank had contributed to CPP — they could split the entire amount of their CPP benefits. Frank's benefit would drop while Nancy's would increase. This would result in Frank's moving to a lower tax bracket, and there would be an overall reduction in the amount of tax they would have to pay as a family.

In order to split your CPP benefits with your spouse, you must both be 60 or older and apply for your CPP benefits at the same time. The amount you can split is the number of years you've been married, expressed as a percentage of the total years of CPP contributions.

> Candy and Taylor Dulford have been married for 20 years and Taylor has contributed to CPP for 25 years. The Dulfords can split up to 80 percent of their benefits (20 [years of marriage] ÷ 25 [years of contribution] x 100 = 80%). The total amount eligible for splitting will be divided equally between Candy and Taylor.

PROVINCIAL INCOME SUPPLEMENTS

Several provinces/territories provide additional benefits to supplement the federal OAS system. To find out what provincial income supplement or support programs are applicable to your circumstances, contact the provincial government department that handles those matters. See the blue pages of your telephone directory for the number.

WAR VETERAN'S ALLOWANCE

If you meet war service, age, residency, and financial requirements, you may be eligible for various forms of assistance. Widows of former servicemen, too, may benefit. Contact the Department of Veterans Affairs for more information.

- -

It has become clear over the past two or three budgets that we cannot rely on the government to see us through our retirements. Both our Old Age Security and our Age Tax Credit are now means tested. Translation: *if you have the means, you don't get the money*. Since our population of retirees is growing — it's been estimated that by 2032, 7.5 million Canadians will be over the age of 65 — the reality of retirement may mean that fewer and fewer people qualify for government aid.

We have to take personal responsibility for our retirement years by putting a plan in place to ensure our own financial security. And we have to start now. Every year of delay is a year of lost compounding return, less money in retirement, and a lower standard of living.

- -

CORPORATE PENSIONS

WHAT IS A REGISTERED PENSION PLAN?

Registered pension plans (RPPs) are employer-sponsored retirement plans that are accepted by Revenue Canada for registration under the Income Tax Act. RPPs can be broken into two types: contributory and non-contributory pension plans. A contributory pension plan is one in which both the employee and the employer pay part of the contributions to the plan. A non-contribution plan is one in which the employer pays all the contributions.

The rate of participation in RPPs initially increased but has since fallen off. In 1960 only 19 percent of all Canadians between the ages of 18 and 64 belonged to an RPP. At its peak, participation was about 48 percent. However, between 1991 and 1993, only one-third of tax filers participated in an RPP — about the same number as those who regularly contribute to an RRSP. Statistics Canada believes participation in RPPs will continue to decrease because:

- RPPs have become increasingly complicated and, therefore, unattractive to employees because of the changes in legislation governing them.

- As the economy continues to restructure, fewer employees will participate in company-sponsored plans. This is primarily because there has been a significant decline in employment in larger companies — those that traditionally sponsor RPPs.

WHAT ARE DEFINED BENEFIT PLANS?

Defined benefit plans (DBPs) incorporate a promise to pay to retired employees a regular income stream calculated according to a predetermined formula. The employer (also referred to as the sponsor) carries the risk of the promise. With this type of plan, members know exactly how much they will receive at retirement. Due to increasing complexity of DBP legislation, there will likely be a shift from DBPs to other types of pension plans as employers — particularly small and mid-sized companies — choose less complicated options as part of their benefits packages.

WHAT ARE DEFINED CONTRIBUTION PLANS?

Defined contribution plans (DCPs), also referred to as money purchase plans, define the annual contributions required by the employer (and in many cases by the employee). The size of the pension depends on the amount of money accumulated through contributions and earnings in the plan. In theory, at retirement the best pension possible is bought with the funds that have accumulated in the plan.

WHAT IS A DEFERRED PROFIT-SHARING PLAN?

A deferred profit-sharing plan (DPSP) is a trust arrangement registered under the Income Tax Act whereby an employer contributes a portion of the company's profits for the benefit of employees. Contributions are based on an employee's wage and length of service, and benefits depend on how much has accumulated in the plan. Employees are not allowed to make contributions to a DPSP.

GETTING AN ESTIMATE OF YOUR CORPORATE PENSION

If you will be receiving benefits as a member of a company pension plan, you should find out exactly how it works (if you don't already know) and what pension and other benefits you will be entitled to. Request estimates based on different retirement dates so that you can analyze the impact of taking retirement earlier or later.

Make sure that both you and your spouse have a good understanding of these benefits. Will your plan continue to pay your spouse an income after you die? Some company pensions end with the death of the pensioner. Others pay a reduced percentage to the surviving spouse. If there is no continuation of income, or if that income will be reduced significantly, both of you will have to make some decisions about how you structure your other sources of retirement income (such as income from your RRSPs, RRIFs, or annuities).

Is your pension indexed? Inflation can eat away at your pension benefits. Check to see if your pension provides for full or partial indexing, and find out when that indexing kicks in. Also check to see if your company plan is integrated. In other words, will your company benefits be blended with CPP to provide your income?

> Tommy's company pension plan promised to provide him with $1,200 monthly. His plan is integrated with CPP. If Tommy's maximum monthly benefit from CPP is $650, he will receive one cheque for $650 from the government and another from the company for $550, for a total of $1,200.

If your company pension plan is integrated, whenever you get pension income estimates from your employer, ensure these are the "integrated" amounts, so that you don't double-count your CPP benefits.

If your integrated-plan benefits are reduced once you start receiving OAS, make sure that if your OAS is clawed back you would not be losing out twice. Have a chat with the plan administrator to check the likelihood of this and then discuss how to avoid the problem with your employer.

Check to see if your existing benefit programs continue into retirement. Will your health and life insurance remain intact? Do your benefits include a dental plan? Extended health care? Find out where you stand, then make provision for these items yourself if you are not covered when you retire.

Following is a list of questions you can use to help identify the important features of your company pension plan.

CHECKING UP ON YOUR COMPANY PENSION PLAN

1. What types of plans does your company offer? Do you have a choice? Will that choice make a difference in the amount of retirement income you could collect?

2. Is there an eligibility period to belong to your pension plan? Do you have to participate? Do you have to make contributions? If so, how much? When does the plan vest so that you will be entitled to all your employer's contributions? Can you make contributions above those required? Can you buy more pension credits to increase your income during retirement?

3. What happens if you leave the company? Can the pension remain intact? Can you take it with you? Can it be transferred to a locked-in RRSP? What happens to the employer's contributions? To your contributions?

4. How much income will you receive if you stay with the plan until retirement? Will your entitlement be affected by government pensions? What happens if you retire early? Retire later? What's the earliest date you could retire with full benefits?

5. Is your pension indexed to provide protection against inflation? When does indexing begin?

6. What happens if you die before you retire? After you retire? Does your spouse receive benefits? Are those benefits reduced in any way? Does your plan offer any income flexibility?

7. What happens if your marital status changes? Will your pension credits be split automatically? Will a new spouse be eligible for your pension?

8. If early retirement is encouraged or available, how will it affect your short-term (up to age 65) and long-term (after age 65) income? If your plan is integrated, will the company pay the CPP portion until you apply for benefits? Will your company increase your pension benefits to cover the amount you would have received if you had waited until 65 to claim your CPP benefits?

CAN I UPGRADE MY COMPANY PENSION BENEFITS?

If there are years when you were employed by your company but did not participate in the pension plan, you may be able to buy additional benefits for those years. You may also be able to upgrade your benefits. Keep in mind that buying additional pension benefits will have an impact on your RRSP contribution limit and may create an over-contribution.

If you pay cash to buy additional benefits for years of service prior to 1990, you should be able to deduct your contribution at the rate of $3,500 per year. For the years after 1989, you'll be restricted by how much you've contributed to your RRSP. Your plan administrator should be able to guide you through the process of upgrading your pension benefits.

● ●

If you don't have the cash to buy additional years of service, consider transferring funds from your RRSP to the plan to buy the upgrade. Since employers must usually finance at least half of the benefits that will eventually be paid to you, this makes the transfer a very good idea.

● ●

WHAT IS AN RRSP?

A registered retirement savings plan (RRSP) is a tax-deferral plan registered with Revenue Canada into which you can contribute a portion of your earned income (subject to limitations) and claim that contribution as a tax deduction. All income generated by the investments inside an RRSP remain tax deferred until money is withdrawn from the plan. RRSPs allow Canadians to accumulate a much larger investment for their retirement than they could be investing outside an RRSP.

Participation in RRSPs, and the amounts that can be contributed, have increased dramatically since they were created in 1957 by the federal government. Fourteen years after their introduction, only two percent of the population between 18 and 70 contributed. In 1968 less than $175 million had been contributed. However, by 1988, 22 percent had contributed, and average contributions had grown from $900 per contributor in 1970 to almost $2,800 in 1988 for total contributions of $30.3 billion. Total contributions hit $148 billion at the end of 1992 and were up to $230 billion by March 1994. This growth was due to a number of factors, including increases in the contribution limits, greater participation in the workforce by women, strong marketing focus by RRSP providers — which raised Canadian awareness of the benefits of these plans — and the ability to roll over amounts and carry forward unused deduction room.

WHY SHOULD I INVEST IN AN RRSP?

Would you like to be able to maintain your current standard of living when you retire? Most people answer with a resounding "Yes!" After all, you've probably delayed doing quite a few things until retirement. The last thing you'll want is to find that you can't *afford* to do them once you finally have the *time*.

There's been much controversy about whether or not there'll be sufficient government pension money to meet everyone's needs when the baby boomers finally retire. Even if there is, that's not likely to provide enough income. In 1996, combined income from CPP and OAS was about $13,374 — or a little over $1,114 a month — and that's taxable!

If you're lucky enough to belong to a company pension plan, you'll only get a percentage of your current income. Most plans pay a maximum of 70 percent of your pre-retirement income.

Surprisingly, less than 50 percent of Canadians are actively saving for retirement. According to Statistics Canada, only 29 percent of Canadians make regular contributions to an RRSP. Of those who do, 40 percent have less than $10,000 in a plan and only seven percent have over $25,000 in an RRSP. Retirement may come as an awful shock to those who aren't saving now. Without a plan for the future, retirement may be uncomfortable and unrewarding. According to Statistics Canada, more than 40 percent of people over 65 rely on the GIS to see them through retirement. This means that more than 40 percent of retirees have an income of less than $11,000 — *below the poverty line.*

· ·

Interestingly enough, when surveyed, almost every Canadian says that retirement planning is "very important." While over 75 percent expect to maintain or improve their standards of living during retirement, fewer than 15 percent are actually implementing a retirement plan. So the question is, "Where do the other 85 percent of Canadians expect their retirement income to come from?"

· ·

If you want to be financially independent, you need to start saving and investing as early as possible. The longer you wait to start, the more you need to put away each year, so the higher the cost to your cash flow.

As you move closer to retirement, you should be looking for ways to maximize the growth of your RRSPs. Make your maximum contribution each year. Look at the investments you are holding and determine how you could increase your return without substantially increasing your exposure to risk.

It is important to note that your RRSP assets must be converted to a retirement-income option or cashed in by the end of the year you turn 69. The 1996 federal budget changed the maturity date for RRSPs. RRSPs must now mature at age 69 instead of 71. People who turned 69 or 70 in 1996 have to mature their plans in 1997. Those who were 71 in 1996 had to mature their RRSPs by December 31 of 1996. Failure to convert your RRSPs will result in all of them being included in your income and becoming taxable at your marginal tax rate.

• •

For more information on RRSPs, check at your local bookstore for a copy of my *RRSP Answer Book*.

• •

WHAT'S THE DIFFERENCE BETWEEN MY *MARGINAL* TAX RATE AND MY *EFFECTIVE* TAX RATE?

Income	Tax Rate
≤ $29,600	26%
$29,600 to $59,100	41%
≥ $59,100	49%

Your marginal tax rate is the rate of tax you pay on the last dollar you earn. Let's assume the following tax rates:

If you earn $35,000 a year, then you will pay 41 percent tax on your income above $29,600. That means your marginal tax rate is 41 percent.

Your effective tax rate is the average amount of tax you pay. Assuming once again that you earn $35,000 a year, you'll pay 26 percent on the first $29,600 (or $7,696 in tax) and 41 percent on the remaining $5,400 (or $2,214 in tax) for a total tax bill of $9,910 and an average or effective tax rate of 28.31 percent.

NON-REGISTERED INVESTMENTS

Aside from your registered investments (in your RRSPs), you may also have a portfolio of investments that are unregistered. Perhaps you have been buying Canada Savings Bonds through a payroll deduction plan. Maybe you've been investing in mutual funds. Or perhaps you have GICs, or a rental property or two, which can provide a regular income. These investments can provide you with the additional income you need to supplement your pension and RRSP/RRIF income and make all your retirement dreams a reality.

ASSETS

These are all the things you currently own that you could sell to supplement your income. For example, you may have a cottage that has become too much work and that you do not intend to use actively during retirement. Perhaps you've tired of your stamp, coin, or antique collecting. Whatever your assets are, you should take a good look at what you could realistically get for them (as opposed to their appraised value) if you chose to sell them.

PREPARING A NET-WORTH STATEMENT

There's no better way to get a big-picture perspective of your financial position than by completing a net-worth statement. As part of your initial planning, complete the statement provided on page 41 so that you can clearly see, in black and white, just where you stand financially.

A word of warning: try to be as realistic as possible about the value of your assets. People have a tendency to overestimate the value of their possessions because a certain sentimental value is often unconsciously included. However, a purchaser won't have your attachment and will be ruthless in his evaluation.

Start by listing your assets. That will include your cash on hand, savings and chequing accounts, and money on deposit. Check the value of investments such as stocks, bonds, and mutual funds in the financial section of the newspaper or with a broker. The cash-surrender value of your insurance should be stated in your policy. To estimate cars, boats, and trailers, refer to comparables in the

NET-WORTH STATEMENT

Assets (what you own)

Chequing/savings account(s)	$
Investments (mutual funds, GICs, etc.)	$
Value of home	$
Value of other property	$
Automobile(s)	$
Cash value of life insurance	$
RRSP(s)	$
Business interests	$
Other	
Total Assets	$

Liabilities (what you owe)

Mortgage(s)	$
Loan(s)	$
Personal line(s) of credit	$
Credit card(s)	$
Unpaid bills	$
Taxes owed	$
Other debts	$
Total Liabilities	$

Net Worth (assets – liabilities) $

classifieds. And remember, while you paid the retail price for many of your possessions, you'll likely only receive the wholesale value if you decide to sell them.

Now add up everything you owe. This will include your mortgage, outstanding balances on your line of credit and credit cards, and any loans you may have. It'll also include yet-to-be-paid bills (referred to as your "accounts payable"), as well as taxes owing.

Subtract your total liabilities from your total assets and you have your net worth.

It's highly unlikely that you're going to sell everything you own to realize your net worth in cold hard cash. However, completing a net-worth statement is useful in helping you review your investment decisions.

Once you've determined your net worth, look back at your assets. Are you satisfied with their quality? Are they earning the return you expected? Are you satisfied with your total asset base? Perhaps you have a large amount of cash in a savings account. By moving that money to a term deposit or money market fund you'll very likely earn a higher rate of return.

Now, have a look at your liabilities. Are you paying the lowest possible interest? Can you renegotiate? How quickly can you eliminate these debts? Perhaps you have an investment that is not doing particularly well and that you could sell to eliminate all or a part of your debt. Even a small payment toward your mortgage principal will save you thousands of dollars in interest over the long term.

If you have a low-return investment (say, a GIC earning five percent) and a high-cost credit balance (your Sears card has a balance and you're paying exorbitant interest), you'll be way better off cashing in your pre-tax GIC to pay off your post-tax Sear's card.

At this point, you may want to seek help from a financial adviser so that you can ensure your financial position meets your retirement objectives.

PREPARING FOR RETIREMENT

How far are you from retirement? Do you think a little future-gazing will do you some good? Perhaps you don't plan to retire for another 20 years. Maybe you'll be retired within the next five years. A look at where you are and where you need to be financially can only help ease your way into retirement. The earlier you start, the more likely you are to reach your goals. Early planning lets you anticipate and adapt to the changes that occur as your lifestyle changes.

If you're younger than 69 (or have a spouse younger than 69) you can still contribute to an RRSP to continue accumulating assets that can provide a retirement income. At the pre-retirement stage, you may also have debts such as a mortgage, a car loan, or a personal line of credit that you can work to eliminate or at least minimize before you begin living on a fixed income. You also have to look at your current investments and make some adjustments to the levels of risk, return, and liquidity in relation to your age and time left to retirement. And, of course, you'll need to think about what it will cost to live during retirement, how much income you'll have from your various sources of pension, and how you'll make up the difference from your registered and non-registered investment assets.

PRIORITIZING YOUR RETIREMENT OBJECTIVES

If you find you have to live on considerably less than you have been used to, you'll need to prioritize your objectives to ensure you can still do the things that are most important to you. Begin by identifying the things that are central to your life. Then ask yourself what you can whittle away. You may be willing to be less of a clotheshorse if you can spend more on travelling. Or you might swap an expensive hobby for one with fewer financial strings.

To decide which things are most important, make a list of all the things you want to do during your retirement. Write down all your dreams: the trips you've been planning for years, the kind of car you want to drive, the people you want to visit.

Next, use a forced-choice method to prioritize your list:

- Compare the first item on your list with the second. Place a check mark beside the one that is most important. Continue to rate the first item against each of the others on your list, each time placing a check mark beside the one you feel is most important.

- Start the whole exercise again, this time rating the second item against all the rest on your list.

- Keep going until you've compared your final two items. When you are finished, you will have ranked your objectives in order of priority. The one with the most check marks will be the most important.

- The final step is to put a dollar value on each of your priorities. You can move as far down the list of your objectives as your retirement income will take you.

This method of making a decision may seem tedious at first, but it's tried and true within the financial-planning world. And it will stop you from running off on a whim only to find you're somewhere you really don't want to be, doing something you really don't want to do.

ESTIMATING YOUR RETIREMENT INCOME

As you read earlier, your retirement income will come from a variety of sources: government pensions, employer-sponsored pensions, personal retirement savings, unregistered investments, and the sale of assets. Complete the Retirement Income worksheet on page 45. You and your spouse should keep your figures separate to ensure that, when you get into a discussion of how much either one of you will have individually, you'll have a point of reference. You'll also need to have separate figures to calculate your income tax. (Remember, the first $1,000 in pension income is tax free because of the pension income tax credit.)

Once you've calculated your gross income, you'll have to estimate how much tax is payable on your income. Check with Revenue Canada to see what the most current income tax brackets are for your province. If you only want to do an approximation, you can use the figures on page 39.

ESTIMATING YOUR RETIREMENT EXPENSES

In order to retire *when* you want, and to live the *way* you want during retirement, you have to know just what it will cost to live. The best way to calculate this is to do a budget for what you're spending

RETIREMENT INCOME
Sources of Regular Monthly Income

Government-sponsored	Self	Spouse
Canada/Quebec Pension Plan	$	$
Old Age Security	$	$
Spousal Allowance	$	$
Guaranteed Income Supplement	$	$
Survivor's Benefits	$	$
Provincial Income Supplement	$	$
Other	$	$

Employer-sponsored		
Private employer pension(s)/DPSP	$	$

Individual Registered Savings		
Income from RRSPs	$	$
Income from RRIFs	$	$
Income from annuities	$	$

Individual Unregistered Investments		
Term deposit/GIC interest	$	$
Savings account interest	$	$
Treasury bills/money market funds interest	$	$
Bond/mortgage interest	$	$
Dividends from stocks or mutual funds	$	$
Income from real estate	$	$
Other	$	$

Employment Income (part-time or full-time)	$	$

Total Income	$	$
Less estimated income tax (see page 39)	$	$
Less OAS clawback (see pages 26-28)	$	$
Total Net Income	$	$
Total Joint Income	$	

now, and then project what it will cost when you move into retirement. Naturally, some costs will go down. You'll likely spend less on clothing and daily transportation, since you'll no longer need to get to work or look good when you get there.

Remember to tell your car-insurance company when you retire, because people who use their cars only for pleasure pay less insurance.

As your children leave home, you'll find your household expenses declining. You will probably have acquired most of the "big stuff" you need prior to retirement. And with a well-planned financial strategy, you'll also likely have eliminated your mortgage. It's also very likely that you'll pay tax at a lower rate, since your income will likely be reduced. However, other expenses will increase. Premiums on life and health insurance will increase, as will your costs for medication and dental care. And if you plan an active retirement, it's very likely that your travel and entertainment costs may rise.

DON'T FORGET YOUR EMERGENCY FUND

An emergency fund is used to meet unexpected expenses. Financial media often talk about emergency funds in the context of unforeseen unemployment. However, *everyone* should have an emergency fund. Whether the emergency is unforeseen medical expenses not covered by insurance or a new roof, an unexpected big bill can put a serious crimp in your budget.

The size of your emergency fund will depend on your financial commitments and the amount of income you have regularly flowing in. If it looks like things may be tight during retirement, establish a fairly significant emergency fund before you retire. If you know for certain that you will have more income than you'll need, your emergency fund can be smaller. Also consider the source of your income. A pension that is indexed is more reliable than income from interest-bearing investments, since a decline in interest rates could mean significantly less income.

Once you have your emergency fund set up, keep it in conservative, highly liquid assets. There's no point in having an emergency fund in a five-year GIC where you can't get at it. A money market fund is a safe bet.

If the idea of having $10,000 sitting in a money market fund earning a low rate of interest makes your blood run cold, the following strategy may be for you. First, apply for a personal line of credit equal to your emergency fund. Next, invest your emergency fund as you would any other investment dollars. (Okay, okay, perhaps with a little less risk.) In the best-case scenario, should you need to access your emergency fund, your investments will be at their all-time high and you can sell them, reap a nice capital gain, and cover your emergency. However, should the timing be all wrong for liquidating your investment, you could buy yourself the time to let your investment do its thing by first calling on your personal line of credit.

Whichever route you choose, make sure you build an emergency fund into your budget for unforeseen expenses. Even if you plan a tranquil retirement, unexpected expenses can mess up your budget. Be prepared.

An Estimate of Expenses worksheet is provided on pages 48-49. Fill in this worksheet using your current expenses in the left column. These figures represent your monthly costs in after-tax dollars. Fill in your anticipated expenses during retirement in the right column. The more the amounts in the right column exceed your current expenses, the more money you'll have to invest in your retirement savings program to achieve your retirement goals.

Since all the figures produced so far have been calculated in "today's dollars," you'll also have to make some adjustments for inflation.

HOW WILL INFLATION AFFECT MY BUDGET?

Most people have heard how inflation eats away at our money. In 1965, a litre of milk cost 33 cents. By 1990, the price of a litre of milk had risen to $1.39 — a 421-percent increase. The price of a litre of gas went from 9 cents in 1965 to 50 cents in 1990 — an increase of 555 percent. And the average passenger car went from $4,300 to $15,000 — an increase of 348 percent.

ESTIMATE OF EXPENSES

For annual amounts such as insurance and car licence, divide the yearly amount by 12.

	Estimated Monthly Expenses	
	Now	After Retirement
Housing		
Rent or mortgage payment (and condo fees)	$	$
Property taxes (municipal, school, water, etc.)	$	$
Electricity	$	$
Heat	$	$
Maintenance and repairs (service contracts)	$	$
Cable	$	$
Telephone	$	$
Insurance (fire, liability, contents)	$	$
Vacation Home		
Rent or mortgage payment (and condo fees)	$	$
Property taxes (municipal, school, water, etc.)	$	$
Electricity	$	$
Heat	$	$
Maintenance and repairs (service contracts)	$	$
Cable	$	$
Telephone (long distance)	$	$
Insurance (fire, liability, contents)	$	$
Transportation		
Car payment (loan, lease)	$	$
Gas and oil	$	$
Repairs and maintenance	$	$
Insurance and licence	$	$
Parking	$	$
Public transportation	$	$
Taxi	$	$
Medical & Dental		
Insurance (life & health premiums)	$	$
Expenses (prescription, optometrist, etc.)	$	$

	Estimated Monthly Expenses	
	Now	After Retirement
Living Expenses		
Groceries (food, personal care, cleaning)	$	$
Daily purchases (milk, bread)	$	$
Clothes	$	$
Child care	$	$
Books, subscriptions	$	$
Entertainment (meals, movies, dues, sports)	$	$
Spending money	$	$
Miscellaneous (haircuts, pet care)	$	$
Interests & Hobbies	$	$
Family (gifts, financial aid, etc.)	$	$
Vacation & Travel	$	$
Charitable Donations	$	$
Credit Payments (excluding mortgages)		
Loan(s)	$	$
Credit card(s)	$	$
Store financing	$	$
Other	$	$
Other Expenses		
Legal & accounting	$	$
Club/union dues	$	$
Alimony/child support	$	$
Other	$	$
Contingency Fund		
Emergencies	$	$
Capital expenditures (appliances, car, etc.)	$	$
Savings	$	$
Total Monthly Expenses	**$**	**$**

Consumer prices have increased substantially over the past 30 years, gobbling up over 70 percent of the purchasing power of a dollar. While no one can predict the rate of inflation over the next 30 years, we know it will be with us. To protect ourselves, we have to plan for it.

Assuming that inflation averages seven percent, a litre of milk will cost $2.74 by the year 2000 and $10.58 by 2020. Gas will rise to 98 cents a litre by 2000 and $3.81 by 2020. And the average passenger car will cost almost $30,000 in the year 2000, and almost $115,000 by 2020.

WHAT EXACTLY IS INFLATION?

Inflation can be defined as the decrease in money's purchasing power over time. At an inflation rate of five percent, today's $1,000 will be worth only:

$613.90 in 10 years
$376.90 in 20 years
$231.40 in 30 years

Over the past 40 years, the average annual rate of inflation has been approximately 4.5 percent. While inflation is running below that at the moment, we also have to remember back to the '80s when it raged at 14 percent. It's probably not unrealistic to expect that over the next 40 years inflation levels will be similar to those of the past 40 years.

Inflation's erosive power means that each year it becomes more and more expensive to live — a harrowing thought for someone on a fixed income.

Figure 1 on page 51 will help you to estimate what today's dollar will be worth when you retire and how much income you'll actually need to meet your expenses.

To use Figure 1, follow these steps:

1. Subtract your present age from the age you plan to retire. This will give you the number of years you are away from retirement. Find the number in the "Years" column. For example, if you are 53 and plan to retire at 60, you would be seven years away from retirement. So, you will use the "7" in the "Years" column.

INFLATION EQUIVALENTS OF $1,000

Years	2%	4%	RATE OF INFLATION 6%	8%	10%	12%
1	$1,020.00	$1,040.00	$1,060.00	$1,080.00	$1,100.00	$1,120.00
2	$1,040.40	$1,081.60	$1,123.60	$1,166.40	$1,210.00	$1,254.40
3	$1,061.21	$1,124.86	$1,191.02	$1,259.71	$1,331.00	$1,404.93
4	$1,082.43	$1,169.86	$1,262.48	$1,360.49	$1,464.10	$1,573.52
5	$1,104.08	$1,216.65	$1,338.23	$1,469.33	$1,610.51	$1,762.34
6	$1,126.16	$1,265.32	$1,418.52	$1,586.87	$1,771.56	$1,973.82
7	$1,148.69	$1,315.93	$1,503.63	$1,713.82	$1,948.72	$2,210.68
8	$1,171.66	$1,368.57	$1,593.85	$1,850.93	$2,143.59	$2,475.96
9	$1,195.09	$1,423.31	$1,689.48	$1,999.00	$2,357.95	$2,773.08
10	$1,218.99	$1,480.24	$1,790.85	$2,158.92	$2,593.74	$3,105.85
11	$1,243.37	$1,539.45	$1,898.30	$2,331.64	$2,853.12	$3,478.55
12	$1,268.24	$1,601.03	$2,012.20	$2,518.17	$3,138.43	$3,895.98
13	$1,293.61	$1,665.07	$2,132.93	$2,719.62	$3,452.27	$4,363.49
14	$1,319.48	$1,731.68	$2,260.90	$2,937.19	$3,797.50	$4,887.11
15	$1,345.87	$1,800.94	$2,396.56	$3,172.17	$4,177.25	$5,473.57
16	$1,372.79	$1,872.98	$2,540.35	$3,425.94	$4,594.97	$6,130.39
17	$1,400.24	$1,947.90	$2,692.77	$3,700.02	$5,054.47	$6,866.04
18	$1,428.25	$2,025.82	$2,854.34	$3,996.02	$5,559.92	$7,689.97
19	$1,456.81	$2,106.85	$3,025.60	$4,315.70	$6,115.91	$8,612.76
20	$1,485.95	$2,191.12	$3,207.14	$4,660.96	$6,727.50	$9,646.29
21	$1,515.67	$2,278.77	$3,399.56	$5,033.83	$7,400.25	$10,803.85
22	$1,545.98	$2,369.92	$3,603.54	$5,436.54	$8,140.27	$12,100.31
23	$1,576.90	$2,464.72	$3,819.75	$5,871.46	$8,954.30	$13,552.35
24	$1,608.44	$2,563.30	$4,048.93	$6,341.18	$9,849.73	$15,178.63
25	$1,640.61	$2,665.84	$4,291.87	$6,848.48	$10,834.71	$17,000.06

FIGURE 1

2. Now comes the guesswork. What do you think the average rate of inflation will be over the years until you retire? Make your best guess by looking back over the past years and taking the average. For the sake of our example, let's assume the average rate of inflation will be four percent.

3. How much money, in today's and tomorrow's dollars, will you need? Let's assume that after you completed the Estimate of Expenses worksheet, you discovered you'd need about $2,700 per month when you finally retire. Remember, that's in today's dollars. To translate that into tomorrow's dollars, you have to look at how much that needs to increase over the seven years until you retire.

   Move to the right from "7" in the "Years" column to the "4%" column. This tells you that seven years from now you will need $1,315.93 to buy what $1,000 buys today.

   Multiply $1,315.93 by 2.7 (because you need the equivalent of $2,700 per month) and you'll get $3,553.01. So, you'll need a monthly income of approximately $3,553.

Remember, this is an estimate only. To get an accurate figure, you must have a clear picture of which of your expenses will increase and which will decrease or be eliminated completely. You'll also need to have the correct inflation rate. So, even if you're only one or two years from retirement, there will still be some guesswork involved. Or you may simply want to use an average inflation rate of four or six percent for your calculations.

Don't be put off by a figure that seems impossible to achieve. If anyone had told your grandmother that we'd be paying more than a dollar for a loaf of bread, she wouldn't have believed it. The important point is to be prepared so that the impact of inflation doesn't come as a huge surprise.

· ·

When figuring the impact of inflation, remember that your dollars will also lose value during your retirement. You'll have to live on your fixed income for 10, 20, maybe even 30 years. Work out how much you'll

**need to live toward the end of your retirement to see
how hard your retirement dollars will have to work
to keep pace with inflation.**

FIGURING THE DIFFERENCE

Now that you've estimated your expenses, taking inflation into
account as well as your income based on your current holdings,
you'll need to see if there is a shortfall. Complete the Figuring the
Difference chart below.

FIGURING THE DIFFERENCE

Total Net Joint Income	$
Total Monthly Expenses	$
The Difference	$

If there is an excess, particularly in your early years of retirement,
don't just go out and blow it! Remember the impact of inflation.
Manage your funds carefully so you don't find yourself short later on
due to inflation, a reduction in income because of lower returns, or
the death of your spouse.

In 1987 Patricia Galum invested $60,000 in a five-year GIC
paying nine percent. The resulting income was more than
sufficient to supplement her pension income. However, in
September 1992 when those funds came up for renewal, Mrs.
Galum discovered that the best rate she could get was 4.5
percent. In essence, her investment income had been cut by
half because of a change in economic circumstances.

If there is a shortfall (that is, your retirement expenses are higher
than your retirement income), you'll have to up your ante in terms
of retirement savings to ensure this shortfall is covered when you
move into retirement. Alternatively, you can go back and adjust your
expectations — and expenses — for retirement.

DON'T PANIC

Don't be shocked or upset by the results you come up with. It is quite normal for retirement income to be less than your current income. And since most people require less income to live in retirement, you may still be well within acceptable boundaries. If your expenses seem too high compared with your income, go back over your figures to see if you've made allowances for the following:

- Your mortgage should be paid off by the time you retire.

- Your household costs will decrease when the kids leave home (if they haven't already). Plan to use that money for retirement savings or debt reduction.

- You'll probably have all the plates, chairs, fridges, cars, and so on that you'll ever need. Ensure your retirement planning puts you in this position.

- Contributions to such things as Unemployment Insurance, CPP, and company pensions will end when you retire.

- You'll likely benefit from discounts as a "senior." For example, many retail stores, travel agencies, and entertainment facilities offer discounts to people who are 60-plus. Banks have developed special packages for this growing consumer group. Public transportation is discounted. Shop around, compare prices and discounts, and be demanding.

- Your income tax will likely be lower because your income is lower.

- The first $1,000 of pension income is tax free.

- Many of your work-related expenses such as clothing, transportation, and meals will disappear.

- If you've been running two cars, one may be enough. Think about how often you will be inconvenienced and your access to public transportation. Figure out the total annual savings on maintenance and insurance on the second vehicle. Also, consider how much you could get for the car and what that could buy. Weigh your desire to travel by car versus plane or train.

- Your medical costs may be reduced because of supplemental provincial benefits (although we seem to be losing more and more of these each day). For example, some drugs are covered under provincial health plans for people over 65.

- Your need for life insurance coverage may have declined, so you can reduce this category. Take care in your analysis of this situation. Don't work against your spouse's need to make ends meet should your death significantly reduce his or her income.

BOOSTING YOUR RETIREMENT SAVINGS

If you still don't feel comfortable with the gap between your income and your expenses, take action. Here are some things you can do to boost your retirement savings:

- Rein in your spending. One way to have more to put aside for retirement is to spend less. Review your current expenses and look for ways to eliminate little costs here and there. You'll be surprised at the difference it may make.

- Boost your earnings. Can you take a second job? Are there ways to increase the money currently coming in? Look around for ways to make a little extra money. This goes hand in hand with . . .

- Delay your retirement. The later you retire, the more time you have to save and the more time your money has to grow before you have to start pulling on it. And if you also . . .

- Plan to work during retirement, you'll stretch your retirement savings even further. Do you have an interest or hobby you could turn into a money-maker? Would you consider working part-time in a completely new field? Be creative. Don't underestimate the value of your skills.

- Use your equity. Whether you decide to sell and rent, or use a reverse mortgage, your home equity is a good source of additional retirement income.

- Remember that your retirement savings are made up of both income earned on your savings and also your principal. Does this sound obvious? A lot of people resist drawing on their principal during retirement for fear that they will outlive their money. If necessary, take your figures to a financial adviser who can show you exactly how long your principal will last. And for those of you hell-bent on leaving an estate for your children, who was *your* benefactor?

MAXIMIZING YOUR RETIREMENT NEST EGG

Having looked at what your expenses will be and how much income you'll generate based on your current holdings, you have to ask yourself a couple of questions:

- How long will my retirement assets have to last?
- How much must I save today to have what I need for tomorrow?

HOW LONG WILL MY RETIREMENT ASSETS HAVE TO LAST?

That's a really tough question to answer. Over the past 60 years, life expectancy has increased significantly. In 1931, men were expected to live to 60 and women to 62. Advancements in diet and medical care have pushed life expectancy to 73 for men and almost 80 for women. And life expectancy is expected to rise even further. By the year 2001 it is expected to be 77 for men and 84 for women.

Given the fact that insurance companies are the experts in predicting how long we will live, we can go to life expectancy statistics for a general idea. According to Statistics Canada, 65-year-old men can expect to live another 16 years. Women of the same age have a life expectancy of 85. So you could buy a fixed-term annuity that pays you to age 90 and you might be covered. But what if you live to be 91 or 95 or 97? The likelihood of that is increasing every day because of better health care, differences in lifestyle, and new drugs. In fact, Statistics Canada's figures show that the number of people attaining the ripe old age of 100 will increase dramatically. Maybe a RRIF or life annuity, both of which provide an income for your full lifetime, would make more sense if your family has a history of longevity.

If you retire at 60, which loads of people do, you could have more than a third of your life still ahead of you. So, careful planning is definitely needed to ensure you don't outlive your assets. Keep in mind that as you grow older, your income needs will likely taper off. Most people slow down after 75, and with less activity comes less expense.

Having decided you're going to have a long and active retirement, you may decide you need to up the ante in terms of how much you put away for the future.

HOW MUCH SHOULD I SAVE EACH YEAR?

There's a direct correlation between age and the amount of assets accumulated. In his book *Canadian People Patterns*, Roger Sauvé shows that on average, if you're 25, the value of your household assets is somewhere around $14,000. By the time you hit 35, you'll likely have assets of about $60,000, and by the age of 44 your assets will have grown to about $107,000, peaking at age 64 at about $144,000. Most Canadians build their assets slowly as they get older, and their debt levels are quite high when they're in their mid-forties.

However, a higher focus on the building of assets, particularly for retirement purposes, may be just around the corner. Much has been written about Canadians taking personal responsibility for their retirement savings. The government has put the emphasis on the individual for retirement planning by providing tax incentives for taking care of the future. And it is very likely that our government pension systems will undergo significant changes as the population ages and there are fewer workers to support more retirees.

Unfortunately, the longer we wait to start, the harder it is to put away as much as necessary to accumulate the final goal. In his book *Economic Security in an Aging Population*, actuary Robert Brown estimates that if you start saving when you're 25 and plan to retire at 65, you'll need to save between four and five percent of your gross income in order to end up with approximately 70 percent of the average industrial wage (which is now about $30,000). If you wait until age 35 to start, you'll need to put away between six and eight percent of your income. And if you hold out till you're 45, you'll need to save between 12 and 14 percent. If you want to retire with a higher standard of living, you'll have to save even more.

Figure 2 on the following page shows how much you must save each year, depending on how close you are to retirement, for each $1,000 in assets you wish to have.

How Much Should I Save?

This chart shows how much you must save each year to build $1,000 of retirement capital.

Years To go	If your RRSP grows at this rate					
	7%	8%	9%	10%	11%	12%
5	173.89	170.46	167.09	163.80	160.57	157.41
10	72.38	69.03	65.82	62.75	59.8	56.98
15	39.79	36.83	34.06	31.47	29.07	26.82
20	24.39	21.85	19.55	17.46	15.58	13.38
25	15.81	13.68	11.81	10.17	8.74	7.50
30	10.59	8.83	7.34	6.08	5.02	4.14
35	7.23	5.80	4.64	3.69	2.93	2.32
40	5.01	3.86	2.96	2.26	1.72	1.30

Figure 2

Let's say you currently earn $60,000 and are 45 years old with 15 years until retirement. Through your retirement income and expenses calculations, you've decided that you'll need about $42,000 a year (in today's dollars) to live comfortably. Let's also say that inflation is running at four percent. That means you'll need approximately $76,000 in annual income after retirement. Your current income statement shows that with your company pension plan, government pensions, and your existing RRSP savings, you can predict an income of about $42,000. You'll need to make up the difference of approximately $34,000. At an annual return of 10 percent, you'll need retirement capital of approximately $340,000. Assuming you earn an average of 11 percent a year on your RRSP over the 15 years, this means you'll need to put away $9,884 ($29.07 x 340) each year.

WHAT A DIFFERENCE A FEW PERCENTAGE POINTS CAN MAKE

Two percent may not sound like much, but it is. Over time, even a small difference in your rate of return can have a tremendous impact on the growth of your investment. The chart on the following page shows the difference in growth for $10,000 invested at various rates of return. As you can see, the differences are significant.

Years	2%	4%	7%	11%
5	$11,040	$12,161	$14,025	$16,851
10	12,189	14,802	19,672	28,394
15	13,459	18,009	27,590	47,846
20	14,859	21,911	38,679	80,623
25	16,406	26,658	54,274	135,855
30	18,114	32,434	76,123	228,923

Assuming you choose a portfolio of investments that gives you only a two percent higher rate of return, over thirty years your investment would earn an extra 78 percent.

If you think these differences are only applicable when you are building your assets, here's more good news. Once you retire and begin to make withdrawals, even a small difference in return can extend the life of your retirement portfolio. For example, a portfolio of $100,000 invested at seven percent, with an annual payout of $12,000, would last approximately 14 years for a total payout of approximately $167,000. By increasing your return just two percent, the same portfolio would last just over 17 years for a total payout of approximately $205,000. With a return of 11 percent, the $100,000 portfolio would last almost 25 years for a total payout of approximately $298,000.

With just a little higher return, you can achieve significantly greater rewards over the long term. And during your retirement, you'll benefit from the very real value even a small increase in performance can provide.

MAKING YOUR MONEY WORK FOR YOU DURING RETIREMENT

Since today's retirees live longer and are more active than any previous generation's, making sure your retirement portfolio continues to work as hard as possible only makes good sense.

TIP #1: USE YOUR UNREGISTERED ASSETS FIRST

Let your RRSP investments continue to grow and use your unregistered assets to supplement your government and corporate pensions. While RRSPs are usually spoken about as a way to save for retirement, they're also a great way to maximize your tax-deferred growth, at least until you reach age 69.

TIP #2: KEEP INVESTING IN YOUR RRSP

As long as you have earned income, you can continue to invest in an RRSP in your name (until you turn 69) or your spouse's name (until he or she turns 69).

TIP #3: DON'T SHY AWAY FROM EQUITIES

Discard the old-fashioned notion that by the time you retire all your investments should be converted from growth to income. As you saw just a little earlier, even a small percentage difference in return can mean years of difference in the life of your retirement portfolio. Historically, stocks have produced a greater than 10 percent return, on average. That's why so many people suggest that you invest a portion of your retirement portfolio in growth-oriented mutual funds. Make sure you continue to diversify your investments. While you may want to move to a more conservative portfolio, resist the urge to eliminate all the stock-based investments. Unless you're starting off with an absolute pot-full of money, you'll need some growth if you want your investments to last at least as long as you do.

TIP #4: MINIMIZE YOUR TAXES

Now that you're living on a fixed income, paying the least amount of tax possible will be more important than ever before. That'll take smart investing and good tax planning. It'll also mean structuring your income flow from your investments so that you pay the least amount of tax possible. For example, you can structure your income to receive your Old Age Security at least every other year. Or you might decide to take your income from your RRIF at the latest possible date so your money can earn tax-deferred income for as long as possible. There are a number of strategies that when used together will minimize your taxes and maximize your retirement income.

SUMMARY

Despite the availability of a number of retirement-income sources, and the incentives provided to save for retirement, many Canadians are still moving into retirement with less than adequate resources to maintain their standard of living. Many have waited too long to start saving for retirement. Others haven't managed to save anything at all. And many people haven't taken into account the impact of inflation. By being prepared, we can all plan more effectively to make our retirement years as magical as we hoped they'd be. And the earlier we start thinking about the issues involved, the better prepared we'll be.

4 RETIREMENT-INCOME OPTIONS

If you're about to retire, choosing the retirement-income option that best meets your needs is a matter of understanding the options and the rules surrounding them. You have to make a decision regarding what to do with your RRSP assets by the end of the year you turn 69. If you don't, the funds cease to be tax-sheltered, and so all contributions and income earned in the plan will immediately become taxable. That means if you have an RRSP worth $100,000 and you don't make your decision by the deadline, you have to declare the full $100,000 as income — and pay tax on it. Ouch!

You have four options when collapsing your RRSPs. You can:
- make a cash withdrawal
- transfer your RRSP assets to a RRIF
- use your RRSP assets to purchase an annuity
- use any combination of the above alternatives.

In choosing a retirement-income option, or combination of options, you should consider carefully how important the following are to you:
- a steady source of income to meet your present retirement needs
- your future needs, taking inflation into account
- your spouse's needs in the event of your death
- minimizing the tax payable on your assets for as long as possible
- the level of control you wish to have over your assets
- meeting special cash needs
- maximizing your estate (i.e., the amount you leave to your beneficiaries when you die)

When planning for your retirement income, you have to take a lot of uncertainties, such as inflation, into account. But with careful planning, you can make allowances for these uncertainties.

CAN I JUST TAKE CASH FROM MY RRSP?

Whenever you withdraw cash from your RRSP, it is fully taxable. Financial institutions are required to withhold tax at source before releasing the funds. The amount of tax withheld is based on the amount withdrawn:

	Canada except Quebec	Quebec
Up to $5,000	10%	21%
$5,001-$15,000	20%	30%
Over $15,000	30%	35%

Some people choose to take cash from their RRSPs, as opposed to using any other alternative, despite the fact that cash withdrawals are fully taxable. Perhaps you are collapsing a small plan. Maybe you have sufficient unregistered investments and pension income to meet your ongoing needs. Or perhaps your RRSP generates sufficient income to meet your immediate needs and you've chosen to pull that income, leaving your principal intact.

Polly Paige decided to take early retirement when she was 59. She chose not to receive income from her company pension plan until she was 65 so she'd get the best benefit. As a part-time nurse, Polly's income is $17,000. However, this year, she figures her expenses will be about $26,000.

Polly has RRSPs totalling $60,000, which will generate an income of $9,000 this year. She decided to withdraw the additional funds she'll need from her RRSP this year to cover her additional expenses. She won't have to touch her principal and can simply take the income out as a cash withdrawal.

WHAT IS A RRIF?

A registered retirement income fund, or RRIF (pronounced "riff"), is the natural extension of an RRSP. While an RRSP exists for the purpose of accumulating tax-sheltered funds for retirement, a RRIF exists for the purpose of making payouts to provide an income during retirement.

Funds transferred to a RRIF remain tax-sheltered and continue earning tax-deferred income for as long as they remain in the plan. RRIF plan-holders, or annuitants, are required to withdraw a minimum amount each year except the year in which the plan is set up.

Until recently, the assets of the RRIF had to be completely paid out by December 31 of the year you turned 90. However, in 1992 the federal government introduced legislation to extend the payout on a RRIF, so that the funds can last the full lifetime of the annuitant, providing only the minimum amount is taken each year.

RRIFs are available through banks, life insurance companies, brokerage firms, credit unions, and trust companies. (For more information on RRIFs see pages 65 to 76.)

WHAT IS AN ANNUITY?

An annuity is an agreement in which you give a financial institution (such as an insurance company, trust company, or bank) a sum of money in return for a promise to provide you with an income of a set amount for a set period. This set period can be for as long as you live. Payments from an annuity are generally fixed and usually paid monthly, and an annuity can be purchased at any age.

There are two basic types of annuities:

- A life annuity, which provides a regular income payout over your entire life or your spouse's life, with or without a residual value being paid to your estate. Life annuities are sold through life insurance companies.

- A fixed-term annuity (FTA), which provides a regular income until the year you, or your spouse if you so choose, reach 90. Residual payments are paid to your estate. FTAs are also referred to as "term certain annuities," and are sold through life insurance companies, and some trust companies and banks. (For more detailed information on annuities, see pages 76 to 83.)

CAN I USE A COMBINATION OF OPTIONS?

You sure can. Sometimes people choose to use a combination of retirement-income options in order to meet all their needs. If, for example, you want a regular fixed source of income, you might choose an annuity for at least a portion of your funds, since the payments are preset and guaranteed. You might also choose an annuity if you do not want to be actively involved in making investment decisions. Annuities are usually very popular during periods of high interest rates, because you can lock in your funds to take advantage of those high rates.

If you're concerned about maintaining your flexibility, you might choose to invest at least a portion of your RRSP money in a RRIF. The same is true if you are concerned about the effects of inflation over the long term or if you wish to maximize your estate.

In the past, many people who were concerned about having an income past age 90 often chose a life annuity to provide this protection. However, with the changes in RRIF legislation, this is no longer necessary. Now, RRIFs can provide an income for your full lifetime.

Before deciding which option, or combination of options, to choose, remember to consider your:

- present and future income needs, allowing for inflation and unusual expenses

- spouse's income needs in the event of your death

- tax circumstances and needs with respect to the value of your estate.

RRIFS IN DETAIL

Since the creation of RRIFs, the growth of this retirement-income option has been significant. As more financial institutions made the product available and marketing efforts increased, more and more people began to choose RRIFs as their option for financing retirement.

RRIFs were first introduced in 1978, but it was not until December 1986 that new legislation was introduced to increase their flexibility, making them more appealing. Prior to 1986, we were only allowed to own one RRIF at a time and could not purchase a RRIF before age 60. Now, however, we can have as many RRIFs as we wish and can buy a RRIF at any time. The investment options available used to be extremely restrictive. Now, in comparison to other retirement-income options, RRIFs offer us the highest level of control over the investment of our assets. The result was that RRIF assets almost doubled in 1986, and again in 1987 and 1988. By the end of 1989, RRIF assets had reached $7.4 billion (from only $1 billion in 1986).

Legislation introduced in early 1992 made RRIFs even more flexible. Before this legislation, RRIFs had to be completely paid out by the end of the year in which we turned 90. Canadians had a general concern about ensuring an income past age 90, and the government responded by changing RRIF legislation. The formula for the minimum amount has been changed to ensure the RRIF's assets will last our full lifetimes.

Each time new legislation has been introduced to make RRIFs more flexible, they have become increasingly attractive. At the end of 1989, RRIFs accounted for 71 percent of funds removed from RRSPs by people over 60. With the recent changes in RRIF legislation extending the payout from a RRIF to the lifetime of the plan-holder, the interest in, and growth of, RRIFs is expected to be dramatic.

Many people are choosing to investigate their retirement-income options earlier than they did in the past. Because withholding taxes apply to RRSP withdrawals but not to the minimum amount withdrawn from a RRIF, a lot of people start "shopping" the retirement-income-options market in their late fifties and early sixties, making the purchase decision well before they reach 69.

WHEN CAN I BUY A RRIF?

A RRIF can be purchased:

- on or before December 31 of the year you turn 69 with funds transferred from an RRSP,

- at any time with funds transferred from another RRIF, and

- at any time with funds from a commuted, or "cashed-in," annuity that has been purchased with RRSP assets.

You can have as many RRIFs as you wish and can transfer these RRIFs from one financial institution to another without tax consequences (using Form T2033), subject to the terms and conditions of the financial institution where the RRIF is held.

A RRIF cannot be purchased with funds from a "locked-in" RRSP.

WHAT IS A LOCKED-IN RRSP?

A locked-in RRSP (sometimes called a locked-in retirement account, or LIRA) is an RRSP with limiting provisions attached to it. It is used when an employee switches employers, taking accumulated pension benefits from the ex-employer's plan before retirement. Locked-in RRSP funds can only be used to purchase a life annuity or life income fund (LIF). For more information on LIFs, see pages 89 to 91.

WHEN CAN I TAKE PAYMENTS FROM MY RRIF?

You can begin receiving income from your RRIF as soon as it's established, but you must begin receiving income no later than the following year. So, if you buy a RRIF in 1999, you can take an income in 1999, but you *must* take an income in the year 2000.

HOW MUCH CAN I TAKE FROM MY RRIF?

There is a legislated annual minimum payout (the "minimum amount") that must be paid from the RRIF each year, with one exception: it is not necessary to take a minimum amount in the year the RRIF is opened. In the year in which the plan is set up, the minimum amount is considered to be nil, or zero.

Because legislation was introduced to change the way the minimum amount is calculated, two rules are in place:
- the minimum-amount formula
- the minimum-amount schedule of percentages

WHAT IS THE MINIMUM-AMOUNT FORMULA?

The formula (see Figure 3) is based on:
- your age (or your spouse's age if you choose, provided you make that decision before the first payment is made),

- the number of years until you turn 90, and

- the value of your plan.

MINIMUM-AMOUNT FORMULA

The value of the RRIF at the beginning of the year

———————————— *divided by* ————————————

90 *minus* the age of the plan-holder (or spouse)
at the beginning of the year

FIGURE 3

On January 1, Francis Fontana's RRIF was worth $165,000. Francis will be 65 on June 1. Therefore, the formula for him looks like this:

$$\frac{\$165,000}{(90 - 64)} = \$6,345.15$$

Francis's wife, Natalia, is 60. If Francis based the payments on Natalia's age, the formula would look like this:

$$\frac{\$165,000}{(90 - 60)} = \$5,500$$

WHAT IS THE MINIMUM-AMOUNT SCHEDULE OF PERCENTAGES?

The minimum-amount schedule of percentages calculation is based on:

- a schedule of percentages (see Figure 4),

- your (or your spouse's) age at the beginning of the year, and

- the value of your RRIF at the beginning of the year.

To calculate your minimum amount using this schedule of percentages, begin by choosing the percentage that corresponds to your age at the beginning of the year. Then multiply that percentage by the value of your RRIF at the beginning of the year.

Carlos Castina will turn 82 on May 11. So, at the beginning of the year he is 81. His RRIF was valued at $45,000 on January 1. Therefore, Carlos's calculation looks like this:

$$8.99\% \times \$45,000 = \$4,045.50$$

This new calculation was introduced so that the level of withdrawals will increase each year until you turn 94, to provide inflation protection. From 94 onward, the minimum payment will be 20 percent of the value of the RRIF funds at the beginning of the year, so that payments may continue for your lifetime.

WHEN DO EACH OF THE RULES APPLY?

Naturally, there are rules about when each calculation is used. The formula calculation shown in Figure 3 applies:
- if you are under 79 and have a "qualifying" RRIF

- if you open a RRIF before you reach 71.

	SCHEDULE OF PERCENTAGES	
AGE	EXISTING RULES	NEW RULES
71	5.26	7.38
72	5.56	7.48
73	5.88	7.59
74	6.25	7.71
75	6.67	7.85
76	7.14	7.99
77	7.69	8.15
78	8.33	8.33
79	9.09	8.53
80	10.00	8.75
81	11.11	8.99
82	12.50	9.27
83	14.29	9.58
84	16.67	9.93
85	20.00	10.33
86	25.00	10.79
87	33.33	11.33
88	50.00	11.96
89	100.00	12.71
90	0.00	13.62
91	0.00	14.73
92	0.00	16.12
93	0.00	17.92
94+	0.00	20.00

FIGURE 4

The schedule of percentages calculation shown in Figure 4 applies:
- if you are 71 or older and have a "non-qualifying" RRIF

- if you are turning 79 or more, regardless of when the RRIF was opened.

WHAT ARE QUALIFYING AND NON-QUALIFYING RRIFS?

RRIFs opened on or before December 31, 1992, are referred to as qualifying RRIFs. To remain qualified, no new RRSP funds can be added to these RRIFs after 1992. Qualifying RRIFs can accept additional property from another qualifying RRIF (that is, transfers between qualifying RRIFs are allowed).

RRIFs opened on or after January 1, 1993, are called non-qualifying RRIFs. If non-qualifying assets (that is, assets converted after 1992) are added to a qualifying RRIF, it would become a non-qualifying RRIF.

On December 21, 1992, Donna Drackmore opened a new RRIF. Donna will be 71 in June. Because she opened her RRIF before January 1, 1993, which is when the new rules came into effect, it is a qualifying RRIF. And since she is under 71, the old calculation would be used.

Donna's sister, Debbie, also has a RRIF, which she opened in 1990. However, in June of next year Debbie will turn 80. That means that at the beginning of next year, Debbie will be 79, so the schedule of percentages calculation will come into effect.

Debbie's husband, Derick, will turn 71 in August of next year. He plans to convert his RRSP to a RRIF in December of this year. Next year he must begin receiving payments from his RRIF. And since he opened his plan after December 31, 1992, and will be over 71 when he begins to take his income, the schedule of percentages calculation will be used.

Derick's younger brother, Dixon, is also planning to convert his RRSP to a RRIF this year, and begin receiving income the next. However, Dixon is only 68. Since he is younger than 71, even though he opened his plan after the new rules came into effect, the formula calculation will be used until he turns 71, at which point the schedule of percentages calculation will come into effect.

HOW CAN I DEFER TAX FOR AS LONG AS POSSIBLE?

Many people are looking for ways to maximize the tax deferral on their registered assets. One way is to base the minimum-amount calculation on a younger spouse's age. Since the lower the age, the lower the percentage used in the calculation of the minimum amount, you can reduce the amount that is required to be withdrawn each year. This will increase the tax-deferral feature of a RRIF. And, since less must be taken, the funds can continue to compound on a tax-deferred basis. It will also extend the life of the RRIF.

If you do not immediately need income from your RRIF, another way to defer your taxes is to take annual payments instead of monthly ones. Taking payments annually means a much higher overall growth in your RRIF assets. That's because of the *magic of compounding interest*. Since the funds remain in the RRIF for a longer period of time, they can earn tax-deferred income longer. The final outcome, then, is a RRIF that typically lasts longer. And if you take that annual payment at the end of the year, you'll maximize your compound growth and minimize your tax position even further.

CAN I TAKE MORE THAN THE MINIMUM?

The RRIF is designed to provide a high degree of payment flexibility. People who choose the minimum usually fall into one of three categories:

1. Those who are required to take income from their RIF due to their age, but wish to minimize their income and, by extension, the amount of tax they have to pay, while maximizing the growth of their assets.

2. Those who want to ensure they don't outlive their income.

3. Those who want their income to be automatically indexed to counteract the impact of inflation.

While you *must* take the minimum amount, you may choose to receive more than the minimum, based on your individual needs for income and your objectives for your estate. However, if you do take more than the minimum, the RRIF assets may not provide enough income for your full lifetime.

When Angela Stevens began thinking about what she would do when she retired, she realized that she would need extra funds early in her retirement to finance her travel plans. Later, she'd need less. When Angela discovered that she could decide how much to take out each year, subject only to the minimum prescribed by law, she decided to open a RRIF. She liked the fact that she was in control, as well as the income flexibility the RRIF offered.

Her brother, Donald, found himself in a completely different situation. Between his company pension plan and the government pensions available, he needed to use only a small amount of his registered assets to meet his early-retirement needs. However, Donald was very concerned about inflation and having sufficient funds to meet his and his wife's needs in the future.

When Donald found out that, if the minimum amount is chosen, a RRIF will pay an increasing percentage each year for his lifetime, thus providing a hedge against inflation, he decided to open one, too. He liked being able to control how much he could take from his RRIF based on his changing income requirements.

HOW OFTEN CAN I TAKE MY INCOME?

As often as the plan you choose allows. When you're looking for a retirement-income option, be it RRIF, LIF, or annuity, you should match the frequency with which you receive your income to your cash-flow needs.

If you'll be using your retirement savings as your main source of retirement income, you might choose a semi-monthly or monthly frequency to provide the same kind of income stream as you received before retirement. If you plan to use your registered assets to supplement your retirement income for such things as quarterly tax payments, a quarterly frequency will do the trick. To meet major expenditures throughout the year such as property taxes, a semi-annual frequency may be perfect. And if you do not need the income and wish to minimize, minimize, minimize your taxes, an annual frequency will fit the bill.

• •

If you're turning 69 and must mature your RRSP, but don't need the income (and the tax), choose an annual payment option and take your payment on the last possible day of the year. You will have maximized the tax-deferred growth of your money (because it stayed in the plan for as long as possible) while still meeting the annual payout requirement.

• •

IS THERE WITHHOLDING TAX ON PAYMENTS FROM A RRIF?

There is no tax withheld at source when only the minimum amount is withdrawn. However, when you make a lump-sum withdrawal or take scheduled payments above the minimum amount, income tax must be withheld. (See page 63 for the percentages withheld.)

> Harold Houdin lives in Calgary. His minimum amount for 1995 is $12,000 (or $1,000 a month). Harold wants to receive $1,500 a month in regularly scheduled payments. The difference between the payments Harold will receive and the minimum amount is $500 ($1,500 − $1,000), so tax is withheld on the $500. Since he lives outside Quebec, 10% tax would be withheld ($50), and so his net payment would be $1,450 each month. If Harold lived in Quebec, the total tax withheld would be 21% ($105), and so his net payment would be $1,395 a month.

Since the minimum amount is considered nil in the year the plan is set up, if you decide to take an income during the first year, the entire income taken is taxable at source.

Often when people are making withdrawals from their RRIFs, they have a specific amount they wish to withdraw. Remember to take into account the tax that must be withheld.

73

Taxes must be withheld when any payments are made to non-residents of Canada. The withholding tax rates for these RRIF payments vary according to the country of residence, and you can check with your financial institution or Revenue Canada for the amounts.

● ●

Regardless of the taxes withheld at source by your pension or on a RRIF withdrawal by your bank, you are responsible for tax on your entire income. Since no tax is withheld on minimum payments from a RRIF, and since other sources of income may also create a tax liability, you'll need to do a projection of your total income for the year in order to estimate the amount of tax you'll be required to remit when you file you tax return or make your tax remittances. Even if no tax is withheld on payments from your RRIF because only the minimum amount is taken, that income is still taxable and will generate a tax liability when you file your next tax return.

● ●

CONVERTING SPOUSAL RRSPS

When a RRIF is set up to receive proceeds from a spousal RRSP, withdrawal restrictions similar to those of a spousal RRSP apply. If contributions were made to *any* spousal RRSP during the year the RRIF is established or the two preceding calendar years, amounts withdrawn in excess of the minimum amount will be taxed in the hands of the contributor — not the spouse.

To avoid income tax having to be paid by the contributor, use caution when establishing a RRIF with funds from a spousal RRSP. If you've made contributions to a spousal RRSP in the year the RRIF is established or the two preceding calendar years, then withdraw only the minimum amount in the first three years of the RRIF. If you think you'll need to take more than the minimum amount from the RRIF, you should stop making contributions to any spousal RRSPs approximately three years before converting to a RRIF.

WHAT HAPPENS TO MY RRIF WHEN I DIE?

There are a number of circumstances that may affect how RRIF assets are distributed upon your death. In all provinces except Quebec, you can designate, or name, a beneficiary by advising the company holding the RRIF and by signing the appropriate form. Everywhere in Canada, you can make beneficiary designations in your will.

If you name your spouse as your beneficiary:

- payments may continue as if your spouse were the annuitant (your spouse would be referred to as "successor annuitant"),

- your spouse may collapse the existing RRIF and set up a new RRIF with new terms and payments,

- your spouse may roll over the RRIF assets into a new RRSP if he or she is under the age of 69, or

- your spouse may collapse the plan and take the proceeds into income (in which case he or she will have to pay tax on that income).

Generally, if the beneficiary is anyone other than your spouse, the plan would be collapsed and a lump-sum payment would be made to your estate. The lump-sum payment would be regarded as your income for tax purposes. The after-tax proceeds would then be distributed to your beneficiaries.

Special rules apply if there is no surviving spouse and you designate a child or grandchild who is financially dependent or dependent because of mental or physical disability as beneficiary under the plan. These types of dependants may roll over the full amount of the RRIF into their own RRSPs, so no tax would have to be paid. Alternatively, they may use the funds to purchase a life annuity, guaranteed-term annuity, or fixed-term annuity.

WHAT TYPES OF INVESTMENTS SHOULD I HOLD IN MY RRIF?

When you establish a RRIF, you'll likely want to ensure the investments you purchase will not only generate sufficient income to satisfy your needs but also keep up with inflation. Whether or not you manage to accomplish this will, in large part, depend on the investments you choose to hold in your RRIF.

Like an RRSP, a RRIF is simply an umbrella for the investments you buy, hold, and sell to provide a retirement income. When you roll over your RRSP assets into a RRIF, you must decide how to continue to invest the money you accumulated in your RRSP. It is the earnings provided by the investments in your RRIF that will allow you to meet your retirement objectives.

Much the same principles apply to managing the investments inside a RRIF as apply to an unregistered investment portfolio. The main difference is that you will likely want not only to earn a good return but also to place a strong emphasis on the preservation of your capital.

Refer to chapter 5 for more information on maximizing your retirement nest egg.

ANNUITIES IN DETAIL

The most common form of annuity is a life annuity, which is available only through life insurance companies. Payments are based on the average life expectancy of a group of people, your health, and current interest rates, as well as a number of other criteria that influence financial projections.

A life annuity offers the security of regular payments for the rest of your life. Payments represent the payout of the lump sum invested and life-expectancy rates in the form of a blend of principal and interest. Payments are made in equal monthly, quarterly, semi-annual, or annual amounts, based on the terms of the annuity contract.

There are two basic life-annuity options to choose from:
- a single, or straight, life annuity, which will pay the agreed-upon income for the life of a single annuitant with no further payments after death.

> At 69, Russell Reid invested $56,000 to buy a single life annuity with monthly payments. However, Russell received only eight payments before he died. At his death, the annuity contract ended and no further payments were made to either his estate or beneficiaries.

Single life annuities aren't the most popular form of annuity. If you don't have a family and don't want to leave an estate, this option may work for you. You may also choose to use a single life annuity in conjunction with a life insurance policy. The income from the life insurance proceeds are tax free on death, so in some cases, this combination can actually work in your beneficiary's favour. However, the difference in income between an annuity with a short guarantee and one that stops when you die can be very small, so it's often in your best interests to go with a guarantee.

- A joint and last survivor annuity is a variation on the single life annuity. It pays a contracted amount of income through the lifetime of both spouses. Payments continue after the death of the first spouse and stop only after the death of the second, at which point nothing further is payable to either the estate or beneficiaries.

  Jackson and Maryann Trevale invested $45,000 to buy a joint and last survivor annuity with monthly payments. Within a year of purchasing the annuity, Jackson died. Maryann lived to the ripe old age of 98. The annuity provided her with a regular monthly income until she died, at which point the payments ended.

Joint and last survivor annuities have a cost associated with them. You usually have to give up about 10 to 15 percent of your monthly income to protect your spouse.

GUARANTEED PERIODS

To protect against losing all the funds in the event of an early death, you can further enhance either of the above life annuities by adding a "guaranteed period." Guaranteed periods range from five to 20 years or until the annuitant(s) turns 90. If you buy a single life annuity with a 15-year guaranteed period and die before the end of the 15 years, payments or their commuted value are paid out to your estate or beneficiaries.

The "commuted value" of an annuity is the equivalent lump sum or "cashed-out" value of future income payments. Typically, the longer the guaranteed period, the lower the annuity payout amount. However, the payout can be so significantly less that it just about always makes sense to have a guaranteed period. In fact, a single life annuity with a guaranteed period can be more cost-effective than a joint and last survivor annuity (see Figure 5).

COMPARING THE PAYOUTS*

Single life, no guarantee. $644.18
Single life, guaranteed 5 years. $623.66
Single life, guaranteed 10 years. $578.21
Single life, guaranteed 15 years. $535.85
Joint life, no guarantee. $529.67
Joint life, guaranteed 5 years. $528.94
Joint life, guaranteed 10 years. $523.51
Joint life, guaranteed 15 years. $511.87

FIGURE 5

*As of June 1990

WHAT IS A FIXED-TERM ANNUITY?

A fixed-term annuity, or FTA, provides regular payments until the year the annuitant turns 90. This annuity can be based on your spouse's age, and payments will continue until your spouse reaches 90. If your spouse is younger, this extends the annuity payments over a longer period of time. At death, payments continue to the surviving spouse until what would have been the annuitant's (or the spouse's) 90th birthday. If the annuitant dies before age 90 and there is no surviving spouse, the residual payments are commuted and paid to the estate.

If you're sure you won't live past 90, an FTA may be just for you. But what if you do? Roughly one out of every six people 65 today will live to 90. Consider carefully your family history, health, and other sources of retirement income before choosing this option.

• •

**A life annuity with a guaranteed period to age 90
pays only a little less than an FTA. But you have the**

security of knowing you'll have an income if you live longer.

• •

WHAT IS A CASHABLE ANNUITY?

A cashable annuity is an annuity that allows full or partial cashing out of all remaining annuity payments. The proceeds can be transferred to a RRIF. Typically, a penalty would be levied on the commutation.

While few companies actively market a cashable annuity, many companies will let you cash in your FTA, because it's relatively easy to calculate the commuted value. Calculating the commuted value on a *life* annuity is a whole different story.

• •

If you discover you're in poor health, or if interest rates are considerably higher than when you bought your FTA, consider cashing it in and purchasing another option.

• •

WHAT IS AN INDEXED ANNUITY?

If you are concerned about inflation or your expenses increasing, you can buy some protection in the form of an indexed annuity. With this option, payments increase by a specific indexing formula, which differs from one company to another. Although you may have to shop around, you should be able to find an indexed annuity that offers one of the following options:

- indexing guaranteed at four percent, compounded annually on your anniversary date

- annual indexing with a rate three percent less than the average yield from federal 90-day treasury bills

- annual indexing of 60 percent of the increase in the consumer price index

- annual indexing of 100 percent of the increase in the consumer price index

With an indexed annuity, you'll receive lower payments in the early years and higher payments in later years. Your initial payments may be 25 to 60 percent less with this option than with a non-indexed option.

WHAT IS AN INCOME-REDUCING ANNUITY?

An income-reducing annuity is a joint annuity that initially provides higher monthly payments, with payments reduced after the death of the first spouse. This usually appeals to people who feel that the surviving spouse will not need as much income as a couple. Income can be reduced by one-third to three-quarters of the original payment amount. Often, the additional income at the beginning of the annuity payout does not balance out with the reduced income at the end of the annuity payout.

WHAT IS A DEFERRED ANNUITY?

While most annuities are purchased to provide an immediate income, a deferred annuity is purchased to provide an income at a future date.

If you find you do not require an immediate income but wish to take advantage of high interest rates, you can use a deferred annuity. Payments can start anywhere from a few months to 10 years from the purchase date. By law, the latest the payments can be deferred is January of your 72nd year. Because your money is generating interest without any payments, the longer you defer receiving payments, the higher the income you'll eventually receive. For example, a $50,000 annuity with a one-month deferral might pay $477. The same annuity deferred for 60 months would pay $856.

WHAT IS AN IMPAIRED ANNUITY?

If you can provide medical evidence that you have a health condition that reduces your life expectancy, you can buy an impaired annuity that rates you as older than you actually are. The result is a higher payment, because the annuity issuer expects to pay for a shorter period of time. You don't usually need to undergo a medical examination. A letter from your doctor detailing your medical condition, history, and treatment is usually enough for the annuity provider.

• •

If you choose an impaired annuity and you are married, remember to take the steps to protect your spouse. While you may initially have to settle for less income, over the long term your spouse will have the income needed. When buying an annuity, you should look at not only your own health but also your spouse's health and what other income-producing assets, apart from the annuity, you have.

• •

WHAT IS A PRESCRIBED ANNUITY?

A prescribed annuity is one that is purchased with "after-tax" dollars. That means the funds used to purchase a prescribed annuity cannot come from an RRSP.

• •

A prescribed annuity and a RRIF can work together to meet your specific needs. If you have unregistered assets that can be used to purchase a prescribed annuity, this will leave your registered assets free for conversion to a RRIF. In this way you can have the security of a fixed, prespecified payment amount provided by the annuity, while maintaining flexibility through the use of a RRIF.

• •

Payments from a prescribed annuity are a blend of principal and interest, and the interest is amortized over the life of the annuity, providing for the same amount of interest income from the annuity each year. This means that you'll end up paying less tax than if you'd invested the same amount in a GIC. For example, if you invested $60,000 in a GIC paying 9.5%, you'd earn $5,700 in interest. If your marginal tax rate is 41%, you'll pay $2,337 in taxes, leaving you with a net income of $3,363. However, if you used that $60,000 to buy a prescribed annuity, your annual income would be $9,540, of which $4,963 would be interest. The rest would be principal and, therefore, untaxable. You'd pay only $2,035 in tax, leaving you with a net income of $7,505.

> **As with other annuities, a prescribed annuity will only provide an income for the contracted period of time. So if you want your money to provide an estate, using a large portion of your assets to purchase a prescribed annuity won't be to your advantage. Of course, you could use a portion of your unregistered assets — say 25 to 40 percent — to purchase a prescribed annuity, and invest the remainder in another option. Alternatively, you could combine a prescribed annuity and a life insurance plan to ensure you have the estate protection you seek.**

WHAT AFFECTS THE PRICE OF AN ANNUITY?

Your age, and your spouse's in the case of a joint and last survivor annuity, is one key factor in determining the annuity payout. Annuity payments are based on mortality tables and the number of years between your current age and your anticipated age at death. This is the approximate length of time annuity payments must last. Everything else being equal, the older you are the higher your annuity payments will be.

Your health is also a consideration. Since mortality is an important factor in determining annuity payouts, an individual with a major health problem may receive an increased payout based on shorter life expectancy.

Annuities are discriminatory! Well, there's a good reason. Statistically, women live longer than men (anywhere from three to seven years). Because of this, women receive lower annuity payouts.

When this factor is combined with a situation where one spouse is much younger than the other, the payment from a joint and last survivor annuity can be substantially lower.

Different types of annuities generate different income payouts. Buying an annuity is like buying a car: the more options you choose, the higher the cost. The options selected all have the effect of lowering the payout. A single, or straight, life annuity has the highest payout.

Most institutions selling annuities employ similar strategies. However, no two are exactly the same. Rates and payments vary widely and you should shop carefully.

The payment from an annuity is, in part, determined by the interest rate in effect when the annuity is purchased. When interest rates are low, think twice before accepting the fixed payout provided by an annuity. You might be better off choosing a RRIF so that you can take advantage of changes in economic conditions. Later, if rates go up and you want a guaranteed steady income, you can always transfer your funds from a RRIF to an annuity and take advantage of those higher rates.

HOW DO RRIFS AND ANNUITIES COMPARE?

For many Canadians, RRIFs are the most popular retirement-income choice. The recent changes in the way the minimum amount is calculated and the extension of the RRIF payout to the full lifetime of the plan-holder will mean even more interest in RRIFs in the future.

The chart on the following page shows many of the important features you may be looking for and whether these features are available on a RRIF or an annuity.

CAN I BUY BOTH A RRIF AND AN ANNUITY?

You sure can, and many people do. You can use an annuity to provide a regular stream of income and a RRIF to cover inflation. Or you can wait until you're no longer comfortable managing your investments and opt for the convenience on annuity offers. When you have to convert from an RRSP (because you've turned 69), you might choose to use a RRIF during periods of low interest, switching to an annuity when rates rise to an acceptable level. You may wish

Features	RRIF	Straight Life Annuity	Joint & Last Survivor Annuity	Fixed-Term Annuity
Lifetime Guaranteed Income	Yes*	Yes	Yes	No
Tax Shelter Benefits	Yes	Yes	Yes	Yes
Opportunity for Maximum Tax Deferral	Yes	No	No	No
Inflation Protection	Yes	No**	No**	No**
Opportunity to Increase Value of the Assets	Yes	No	No	No
Investment Alternatives	Yes	No	No	No
Control over Assets	Yes	No	No	No
Access to Capital if Needed	Yes	No	No	Yes†
Spousal Protection	Yes	No	Yes	Yes
Equal Income Male or Female	Yes	No	No	Yes
Estate Protection	Yes	No***	No***	Yes

* If Minimum Amount chosen

** Unless indexed, no protection from inflation. Indexing varies and will reduce income paid.

*** Some estate protection if purchased with guarantee period. The longer the guaranteed term, the lower the income payments.

† May be limited. Interest-rate penalties apply.

to use your unregistered assets to buy a prescribed annuity and convert your RRSP to a RRIF for maximum flexibility. The fact is, you can divide your money any way you want.

WHAT ARE THE IMPORTANT THINGS TO CONSIDER WHEN THINKING ABOUT MATURING MY RRSP?

Of course, the most important thing will be how soon you'll need to start taking an income from your retirement savings. But there are other considerations too, things like how much you'll need, whether or not you want to use your RRSP savings to provide an estate, and how important tax deferral is for you. On page 86 is a list of questions that will help you to decide your priorities.

WHAT THE NUMBERS MEAN

If you circled mostly 1s in the questionnaire, your RRSP savings will be your primary source of retirement income. You very likely worked hard to save through RRSPs because you knew your company pension plan (if you even had one) wouldn't be enough. Or you may have been self-employed or a member of a group RRSP. You may also be the proud owner of a locked-in retirement account. Whatever the case, you will have clearly accepted the fact that you will be responsible for providing and managing your own retirement income.

Since you'll be depending on your retirement savings for all or most of your retirement income, you should ensure the retirement-income option you choose provides:

- a steady stream of monthly income that will last at least as long as you do (and perhaps as long as your spouse as well)

- the flexibility to design an income stream that meets your specific needs — in terms of both amounts and frequency — as well as the ability to increase or decrease your income as your needs change

- access to additional funds, should the need arise

- protection against inflation

WHAT ARE YOUR PRIORITIES?

Please circle the answer that most closely matches your response to each of the following questions:

	1	2	3
How will you be using your RRSP money?	To meet my day-to-day income needs	For discretionary income to meet special needs	As a long-term tax deferral since I don't need the income
When will you convert your RRSP so you can begin taking a regular income?	As soon as I retire	When I need the money or at 69, which ever is sooner	Not until I have to, at 69
Are you planning to use your RRSP money as part of your estate planning?	If there is money left	With at least a portion of the assets	With as much of the assets as possible
How will you finance your day-to-day cash-flow needs?	Mostly from my RRSP savings	Mostly from my pension or unregistered assets; some from my RRSP	All from my pension and/or unregistered assets
How do you feel about inflation?	I worry that I won't have enough money	I'll probably be fine	Inflation is no problem

- a variety of investment types from which you can choose so you can use an investment strategy that will help you to preserve your capital (to protect your future income) while maximizing your yield (to cover inflation)

- the remaining funds will be taxed at the lowest possible rate.

If you circled mostly 2s, your RRSP savings will be your secondary source of retirement income. You will probably use your RRSP money to supplement the income you receive from other sources. You may want to delay purchasing your retirement-income option for as long as possible, or you may choose to convert a portion of your RRSPs earlier in order to supplement your day-to-day cash-flow needs.

You should probably wait until you're 69 to set up a RRIF. Establishing a RRIF before absolutely necessary means you may be forced to take income when you don't need it. If you find that you do need some of your retirement savings to make ends meet, you can always make a withdrawal from your RRSP. So, stay flexible. Stay in an RRSP for as long as you can.

If you have no other source of pension income (which you need to claim the $1,000 pension income tax credit), then roll only as much as you will need each year to a RRIF (it'll be the $1,000 plus the applicable withholding taxes if the $1,000 is above your minimum annual payout amount) and take the full amount as a lump-sum withdrawal.

Since you will likely have sufficient income from your company and government pension plans to meet your basic needs, your RRSP money will be useful for:

- special needs, such as travel

- supplementing your family's income when pension benefits are reduced due to death of the primary pensioner

- offsetting the impact of inflation on your retirement purchasing power.

Since you won't be depending on your retirement savings for all or most of your retirement income, and you won't be in any rush to make a decision, you can afford to take some extra time to shop around on price. When choosing your retirement-income option, ensure you:

- won't receive income unless you need it, but will have access to your money should an emergency or unexpected income need arise (you may decide to use this money as a source of supplemental income to meet expenses such as quarterly tax payments, annual insurance bills, or periodic water and property tax bills)

- provide protection for your spouse's income after your death if you are the primary income provider.

If you also want your retirement assets to continue to accumulate, then choose an option that will allow you to invest for growth.

If you circled mostly 3s, you have enough money to meet your retirement-income needs, so you don't need to draw on your RRSP savings at all. Your focus will be on minimizing the income you need to withdraw and, by extension, the tax you must pay. Look for a retirement-income option that will let you:

- minimize your income by using your spouse's age (if he or she is younger) for the minimum annual income payment calculation, or by taking the income annually at the end of the year

- maintain your registered holdings for as long as possible to minimize your taxes.

Because of your strong financial position, you can afford to throw your weight around a bit to negotiate for the best rate and, possibly, bonus interest. Consider offering to consolidate your RRSPs when you convert (you likely have a few) in exchange for better rates and/or terms, and *fantastic* service.

Since you don't need this money to provide an income, you should also look carefully at the option's ability to help you in preserving your wealth and providing an estate for your children's benefit.

WHAT IS A LIFE INCOME FUND (LIF)?

When accumulated registered pension plan benefits are transferred from an employer-sponsored plan directly to the employee prior to retirement, those funds must be transferred to a "locked-in" RRSP (also referred to as a locked-in retirement account, or LIRA). This type of RRSP has limiting provisions attached to it. For example, locked-in RRSP funds cannot be withdrawn all at once. These funds can only be used to purchase a life annuity (which we've looked at in detail) or life income fund (which we will look at next) and cannot currently be used to purchase a RRIF. These restrictions are in place to ensure the funds provide a retirement income as originally intended by the pension plan that provided them.

· ·

If you have a locked-in RRSP, don't make any additional contributions to the plan. Open up a new plan for any contributions you wish to make to an RRSP. This will avoid any confusion about which portion of the funds are locked in.

If you have already made additional contributions to a locked-in RRSP, get in touch with the institution administering the plan. Ask them to check their records, and request that they transfer any "new contributions" — contributions made to the plan after the original locked-in funds were transferred in — to a separately registered plan. The last thing you need when you finally retire is to find that all your RRSP assets have been designated as "locked in" and that there are restrictions for their maturity.

· ·

Quebec pioneered the introduction of the LIF as an alternative to an annuity, and most provinces now allow LIFs (the exceptions are P.E.I. and the Northwest Territories). In Alberta and Saskatchewan there is an alternative called a locked-in retirement income fund, or LRIF.

A LIF is very much like a RRIF:

- It functions as a tax deferral option for locked-in funds;

- You maintain control over how your money is invested;

- The assets in the plan remain your assets, to be distributed as you wish;

- There is a set minimum that must be withdrawn each year, and the calculation is the same as with a RRIF. (Unlike with the RRIF minimum payment calculation, you cannot use your younger spouse's age in calculating the minimum annual payment for a LIF.)

However, unlike with a RRIF, there is also a maximum amount that can be taken. The formula for calculating the maximum payout uses an actuarial calculation based on the value of the fund at the beginning of the year, the client's age, and an average government bond yield called a CANSIM rate. This is the same formula applied to a term-certain-to-age-90 annuity, so the maximum you will receive each year is the same amount you would receive if you had bought an annuity-to-age-90.

• •

When transferring from one LIF to another, the maximum income withdrawal for the new LIF funds transferred for that year is zero. So if you intend to take additional income from your LIF prior to the end of the year, you must do so from your existing LIF before it is transferred.

• •

This maximum payout amount ensures that the LIF cannot be completely cashed out, so there is still money in the plan when you reach age 80 and must convert to an annuity.

• •

> **In special circumstances, LIF assets may be paid to you in a lump sum or a series of income payments, providing a medical practitioner gives a written opinion that your life expectancy is likely to be shortened considerably due to mental or physical disability. This is also subject to spousal consent in some provinces. (Not applicable in Quebec.)**

• •

While you can convert (or "annuitize") at any time, since a LIF doesn't require conversion to an annuity until age 80, you can delay annuitizing for up to nine years if the factors aren't in your favour.

WHAT'S DIFFERENT ABOUT THE LRIF?

First, an LRIF does not have to be converted to an annuity. You retain control of the money for as long as you live, and when you die, it goes to a named beneficiary or to your estate. This is of particular interest to those wishing to maintain or build an estate.

Second, while the yearly withdrawal limit for a LIF is based on a term-certain annuity to age 90, the LRIF's maximum withdrawal amount is based on the plan's investment earnings. This maximum is the greater of:

- the investment income accumulated since the plan was opened, or
- the earnings for the prior year.

WHAT IS A REVERSE MORTGAGE?

For many people, a home is their primary capital investment. However, it can be frustrating to be house-rich and cash-flow poor. You may not want to sell your home, choosing instead to remain in a familiar neighbourhood. However, living on a fixed income can mean that maintenance, repairs, and living expenses become just too much to handle.

If you've built up substantial equity in your home, and you're not interested in leaving that equity intact for estate purposes, you may be interested in a reverse mortgage. Using this option, you'll have access to your home equity to supplement your retirement income, while you continue to enjoy living in your home.

Think about a reverse mortgage as the opposite of a conventional mortgage. This option draws on the equity in your home to generate a monthly income. With a reverse mortgage, no interest or principal is due until the home is sold, the reverse mortgage comes due, or the homeowner dies. At this point, if the appreciated value of the property is greater than the amount of the accrued reverse mortgage, the excess goes to the estate. If the value of the property is less than the amount owed, the financial institution that gave you the mortgage has to eat the difference. This is one reason financial institutions don't allow you to use the full value of your home for a reverse mortgage. They limit the amount they will "reverse mortgage" to protect themselves from a decline in the value of your property.

There are two basic types of reverse mortgages: a straight reverse mortgage and a reverse annuity mortgage. With a straight reverse mortgage, you will receive a monthly amount for a specified term that builds a mortgage against your home. When the agreed-upon term has expired (that is, the mortgage comes due), you must repay the mortgage, usually through the sale of the home. If the property has increased in value, you may be able to finance another loan.

With a reverse annuity mortgage, a portion of your equity is used to purchase an annuity with a term that matches the mortgage's. The income you receive (as with any annuity) is based on your life expectancy, sex, marital status, and the prevailing interest rates. When your home is sold or at your death, your estate will receive the difference between the sale price of the home and the income you received from the reverse mortgage. If you live longer than the insurance company expected, you'll continue to receive payments for life. The repayment to the insurance company will come from the proceeds of the sale of the home. Your estate will not be liable for more than that.

Now all this sounds like something for nothing, right? Well, it's not that simple. The fact is, a reverse mortgage is a "rising debt" loan. This means that the total amount you owe grows over time.

Barry and Bev Newsome have finally paid off their home. That house is currently worth $189,000. The Newsomes have decided that to finance their travel plans in the early part of their retirement, they'll use a reverse mortgage to supplement their income. So they assume a reverse mortgage for $30,000 over 10 years at 11 percent and, in return, they receive $250 a month, or $3,000 a year.

While at the end of 10 years Barry and Bev will have received $30,000, they will owe the lender $30,000 *plus the accumulated interest* ($23,970), for a total of $53,970.

In trying to decide if a reverse mortgage is for you, you should think about whether housing prices in your neighbourhood will likely appreciate or depreciate. You'll also have to consider interest rates and the various fees (legal, administration, and so on) associated with the reverse mortgage.

Reverse mortgages may be best suited to those who want to generate some extra income on a temporary basis. These individuals must be prepared to sell their homes in a few years, or have the expectation of an increase in income that will allow them to repay the debt they have built up. Alternatively, individuals who are looking for long-term income must be prepared for the fact that at their death there may be no residual value from the home payable to their estates. If you can live with these facts of life, then a reverse mortgage may be just the ticket to ensuring a comfortable retirement.

5 MAXIMIZING YOUR RETIREMENT NEST EGG

Whether you're using an RRSP to save for retirement or a RRIF to provide retirement income you'll likely want to know what you should be investing in. The same probably holds true for your unregistered investment dollars. Trying to decide which types of investments are best for you can be a difficult task. You have to weigh the return you hope to achieve against the level of risk associated with each specific type of investment. When interest rates are high, the decision seems easy enough. You can buy a GIC at 12 percent, earn a good return, and have all the safety that type of investment offers. But there's even some risk there, and we'll look at that shortly.

Risk and return aren't the only factors that come into play. There are also the issues of minimizing your tax bite, keeping pace with inflation (at the very least), and handling the impact of changes in economic circumstances. The only way to ensure you make the most of your retirement nest egg is to set some clear objectives, learn all about the investments that can help you meet your objectives, take the plunge, and stick to your plan. The issues you should look at include:

- how much safety you need
- your desire for a regular income
- your desire for growth
- how much diversification you're looking for
- whether you're interested in investments with a tax advantage
- how much liquidity you need
- your desire for convenience
- your age
- your investment personality

WHAT'S IMPORTANT TO YOU?

Rank how important each of the following objectives is on a scale of one (low importance) to seven (high importance), using each number only once.

- **Safety**: The value of my initial investment should not fluctuate.

- **Liquidity**: I want to be able to sell my investments on short notice to take care of emergencies or take advantage of investment opportunities.

- **Income**: I need to receive a regular income.

- **Growth**: I want my investments to appreciate significantly over the long term, and I'm prepared to accept some risk to achieve this.

- **Diversification**: It's important that I spread my investments over several alternatives to hedge against a decrease in my portfolio.

- **Tax advantage**: I need investments that will be treated more favourably tax-wise.

- **Convenience**: I don't want to be concerned with day-to-day management of my investments. I want to be able to buy and sell my investments quickly and easily.

Naturally, two or more of these needs may overlap, but in determining which types of investments will best suit your needs, you should try to identify one or two primary needs.

SAFETY

Safety refers to the protection or preservation of capital so that it does not decrease in value. Some people are concerned primarily with ensuring that their initial investment, and the return it generates, is safe. They want guarantees. They want to be sure that on a specific date, they will have exactly what they are expecting.

When you're looking at the issue of safety, you should look at it from three perspectives:

1. The level of volatility associated with the investment. In other words, how much the investment's value will fluctuate over the short term.

2. The level of risk associated with the investment, or the potential for losing the original capital investment.

3. Your emotional safety needs or "investment personality," that is, how much sleep you'll lose worrying about your investments' safety. (See pages 105-110 for more on investment personality.)

Knowing the level of safety you need will help you to determine the asset mix that's right for you.

LIQUIDITY

Liquidity refers to the ease with which an investment can be converted to cash without a significant penalty. A general rule regarding liquidity is: the longer the term, the less the liquidity but the higher the return; the shorter the term, the greater the liquidity but the lower the return.

Liquidity is very important to some people. They may have some extra money they wish to invest; but they may also want to maintain liquidity so that when an opportunity arises, they can take advantage of it. You should maintain liquidity with at least a portion of your money in case of an emergency.

Remember, however, that your money is not working hard for you if it is sitting in a low-interest savings account. In October 1993 many people were not earning even one percent on their savings accounts. When your rate of return is so low, it makes little sense to commit scads of money to these types of accounts.

One way to offset low-interest accounts is to ensure that you receive other benefits for keeping your funds in a particular type of account. Since you need to maintain a high level of liquidity with at least a portion of your money, shop around for an account where the fees will be waived if you maintain a certain balance. For example, some accounts will waive all fees if you keep a minimum monthly balance of $1,000. If you're not earning interest, at the very least you should be eliminating the service charges normally due.

If you're over 55, remember to mention this when shopping for an account. Many financial institutions offer special plans with lower fees or bonus interest to people who are 55, 60, or 65 and older. You may also find yourself benefitting from reduced fees on safety deposit boxes, as well as no-charge traveller's cheques, or free bill payment. Make sure you shop around for the package of features that best suits your needs.

It's quite astounding how much money people have just sitting around, earning little or no return. As one senior told me, "I need to have access to that money. Suppose my kids need help, or I run into an emergency? I can't afford to have my money tied up where I can't get to it."

You don't have to sacrifice flexibility to earn a higher return. Providing you met the minimum investment requirement ($500) in November 1993, you could have earned three percent in a money market fund, while a savings account with the same balance paid only .25 percent. That's right. Just for choosing the right investment product you could have increased your return by 2.75 percentage points. And since money market funds are very, very safe, you wouldn't have had to lose any sleep over the change.

If you have more money, and meet the minimum requirement for a term deposit (usually $1,000), and you're prepared to tie your money up for a minimum of 30 days, you could earn even more. But you have to be prepared to shop around. Rates can vary slightly or significantly, depending on economic circumstances and how hard institutions are fighting for your deposit dollars.

The important thing is to be open-minded, educate yourself on your options, shop around for the best deal, and then take advantage of the options available to you. Don't keep doing things the way you've always done them simply because that's the way you've always done them. Look around for alternatives and take advantage of opportunities as they present themselves.

INCOME

For some investors, maintaining a steady source of income is an important priority. Such income can be used to meet current living expenses or simply to generate cash that can be put into other investment options. Many, particularly those who are older, require investments that generate a regular income that can be used to supplement current or future income needs.

Investment income is received primarily in two forms: interest and dividends. And if you want an opportunity to earn a higher level of income, some trade-off has to be made on security.

Typical income-producing assets include term deposits and mortgages (which earn interest) or preferred shares (which earn dividends). Also consider mutual funds such as bond, mortgage, or dividend-income funds.

GROWTH

Most of us need to increase our investment portfolios to finance our retirement. We can continue to contribute to our RRSPs, and to save and invest outside of our RRSPs, but the fact is, we have only so much disposable income to work with. Unfortunately, we need to spend much of what we earn to make ends meet.

One way of increasing our retirement nest eggs is by investing in options that offer a high level of growth. Making our money grow is what investing is all about. "Growth" refers to the increased value of the original money you invested. For example, if you invest $5 in a stock today and that stock is worth $8 in six months, the difference of $3 is the growth of that stock.

People who are looking for growth opportunities are looking for investments that will, over time, appreciate to a higher level than options such as term deposits or fixed-income mutual funds. If you are one of these people, you must be willing to accept the reduced security of investment that goes with the opportunity for greater return. Traditionally, growth-oriented investors are also usually younger or have substantial funds. However, an individual who has a large holding in fixed-income investments may choose one or two growth investments (also referred to as equity investments) to balance his portfolio — to have more investment scope.

Most growth investors have longer-term objectives and few current income requirements. A typical example is the investor who needs to accumulate a significant amount of capital over, say, a 10-year period to build a retirement portfolio, fund a child's college education, or even purchase a vacation home.

Growth investors most often concentrate on stocks or equity-based mutual funds. The investments they choose depend on their financial goals and their investment personality.

BALANCING INCOME AND GROWTH

Some people want both income and longer-term growth from their investments. While every portfolio should provide a balance of liquidity, income, and growth, the actual weighting of that balance will depend on your personal investment needs. This is referred to in the financial world as "asset allocation."

DIVERSIFICATION

In attempting to balance your investment portfolio, you need to diversify the investments you are holding. Diversification means spreading your money over more than one type of investment (for example, bonds, stocks, GICs, etc.) to provide greater security. In essence, it's the rule about not putting all your eggs in one basket, and the investment world refers to it as "asset mix." The reason asset mix is important is that by purchasing several different investments,

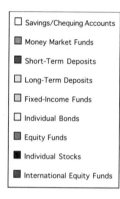

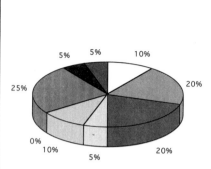

If your investment priorities are liquidity first, growth second, and income third, your portfolio might look like this.

If you are more concerned with income first, liquidity second, with little need for growth, your investment portfolio might look like this.

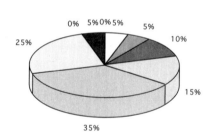

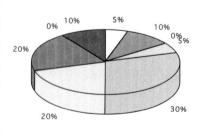

There isn't a single asset mix that's best for everyone. How you mix your assets will be based on your specific investment objectives. Traditionally, however, the asset mix for a conservative person approaching retirement might look like this.

you can reduce your exposure to investment risk. If one of your investments doesn't do particularly well, the others may make up the difference. One low performer is often countered by several other investments that perform on an average or above-average level.

You can diversify your investments — or mix your assets — in many ways. You can do it by the types of investments, using bonds, deposits, stocks, mutual funds, and real estate. You can do it by the quality of your investments, as we mentioned earlier. Or, you can do it by liquidity; you can hold some long-term deposits such as stripped bonds or equity funds, along with some shorter-term investments such as treasury bills. The whole trick to good financial management is finding the asset mix that best suits your needs. And as your age, circumstances, and economic conditions change, so too will the individual investments held in your diversified investment portfolio.

• •

If you are a "small" investor, you may feel you don't have a large enough sum of money to balance and diversify your portfolio. However, you can achieve balance and a comfortable mix of assets by using mutual funds. Mutual funds are one of the greatest financial inventions of our century. They allow you to spread your money, and your risk, among several different investments with as little as $100. And if you buy two or more funds, you can diversify even more.

For more information on mutual funds, see pages 137-152.

• •

TAX ADVANTAGE

Whenever you ask the question "How much tax do you pay?" most people will answer, "Too much." That's why it is so important to have a good understanding of basic tax terms and regulations, and how they relate to investment choices.

Because the Canadian tax system works on the principle that the greater a person's taxable income, the higher the tax rate, the one way to pay less tax is to make the best use of favourable tax treatments. There are several investments that have very beneficial tax treatment. That is, they provide a larger after-tax return because the amount of tax charged against them is lower.

TAX-BENEFITTED INVESTMENTS

- *A capital gain* is the profit earned when an investment such as mutual funds, stocks, or real estate is sold at a price higher than the price paid for the investment.

  It is important to note that if investments that generate a capital gain are held inside an RRSP, any return generated will be tax-sheltered. However, you'll have to pay tax on any gains made when those gains are included in a withdrawal from the RRSP.

  Outside an RRSP, investments that generate a capital gain benefit from special tax considerations — and give you a higher overall return — since you pay tax on only 75 percent of your gain.

  Danny Depase invested in the Canadian Growth Fund. When he sold his mutual fund units, he realized a capital gain of $5,000. Assuming he has a marginal tax rate of 40 percent, the tax payable is:

  $$\$5,000 \times 75\% \times 40\% = \$1,500$$

- *Dividend income* — paid on common and preferred shares — also receives special tax treatment to reflect the fact that Canadian corporations pay those dividends from their after-tax income. Dividend income is grossed up by 25 percent and a dividend tax credit is applied against federal tax payable. The effect is a lower taxation rate for dividend income.

  If Danny Depase invested in Cyplex Odemon shares and received $5,000 in dividend income (assuming a marginal tax rate of 40 percent), the tax payable would be calculated as follows:

Dividend received	$5,000
Gross-up (25% of dividend)	1,250
Total grossed-up dividend	6,250
Federal tax (30% x 6,250)	$1,875
Dividend tax credit (13.33% x 6,250)	833
Net federal tax (1,875 – 883)	992
Provincial tax @ 50% of net federal tax (50% x 992)	$496
Total tax	$1,488

• *Interest income* does not benefit from any special tax treatment, so every dollar in interest earned is taxed at your marginal tax rate.

If Danny Depase invested in a GIC and received $5,000 in interest income (assuming a marginal tax rate of 40 percent), the tax payable would be:

$$\$5,000 \times 40\% = \$2,000$$

Remember, these tax issues are only relevant in the case of non-registered investments. Investments held in an RRSP remain tax deferred for as long as they remain in the plan.

Many other issues regarding your individual circumstances must be considered before you can make a decision about your specific tax situation. Consult your tax adviser.

• •

If you have outstanding debt that is not tax-deductible, make sure you're working to pay off that debt as quickly as possible. Your investment strategy should balance your need to reduce your debt with your need to grow your assets. One good strategy is to use your tax refund from an RRSP contribution to pay off a part of your debt. Always pay off your non-tax-deductible debt first. Your objective should be to be debt free by the time you retire.

• •

CONVENIENCE

Some people want investments that are convenient. In other words, they want to limit the amount of time and effort they need to spend to ensure the investment generates the return desired. That is one of the reasons GICs and term deposits have been so popular. You simply invest your money and you'll receive a fixed return for the term of your investment.

Convenience is also the reason for the growing popularity of mutual funds. Because they are managed professionally, you don't have to worry about making trades to ensure the investment performs to its maximum potential. That's done by the fund managers.

This need for convenience often surfaces in conjunction with many of the other needs we have discussed.

AGE

One final consideration to keep in mind is your age. If you are in your early sixties, almost ready to retire, it is unlikely that you'll want to put the majority of your money in high-growth investments where the risk of losing that money is greater. Instead, you are better off choosing fixed-income investments that would generate a steady return (to provide an income) while offering you a higher level of security.

For those people who are younger, for example in their early thirties, with a longer-term earning potential, depending on your investment objectives, you might choose an asset mix that is weighted more heavily with growth investments. With your higher-earning years still ahead of you, you can afford to make up any losses incurred. As well, any investment in the stock market should be viewed as a long-term commitment. Similarly, people in a younger age bracket will be more interested in longer-term investments.

Depending on your age, financial objectives, and investment time horizon, you have to choose your investment options carefully. Generally, as you get older, you should restructure your registered and unregistered investment portfolios to minimize your risk and maximize the safety of your principal. An investment mix weighted more heavily with income investments provides a greater level of security, pending retirement, when your income will generally be less. As well, since you'll likely need access to your funds to ensure you have sufficient income to meet your day-to-day needs, your investment horizon will also be shorter. Therefore, you should avoid investing in long-term options such as stripped bonds.

Because no single investment offers the perfect opportunity for the highest return, full liquidity, most security, greatest tax advantages, income generation and convenience, you must keep your goals and investment objectives clearly in mind.

TEST YOUR INVESTMENT PERSONALITY

Just as your tax position, income level, and number of years till retirement are important, so, too, is your investment personality. There's no point in making investments that will keep you awake at night. You have to balance the return you want to achieve with your personal comfort level.

Some people are more safety-conscious than others. You need to understand your own feelings about how much risk and volatility you're willing to tolerate — and how much you need to accept — to achieve the returns you desire.

To see where you fit in terms of your investment personality, complete the test on page 106.

WHEN YOU'RE FINISHED . . .

If you circled mostly As and Bs, you're an income-oriented investor. You probably want to generate a steady flow of income from your investments. You're likely to be very concerned about the safety of your investments and feel more comfortable with alternatives such as GICs and Canada Savings Bonds. However, you shouldn't limit yourself to using only those investments you've always used because they are the ones you're comfortable with. Make an effort to learn about other fixed-income investments such as preferred shares, dividend income funds, and mortgage funds. Diversify a little.

If you circled mostly Cs, you're a balanced investor. You likely want to achieve a balance between the income you receive in the form of interest and/or dividends and the opportunity for capital growth. While you're not crazy about risk, you're willing to accept

HOW WELL DO YOU KNOW YOUR OWN INVESTMENT PERSONALITY?

Circle the letter that best reflects how you feel about each of the following statements:

	Not at all			Definitely	
I don't need my investment income to meet my day-to-day living needs.	A	B	C	D	E
I'll accept some fluctuation in the value of my investments in order to achieve higher returns and capital growth.	A	B	C	D	E
I follow the financial markets closely.	A	B	C	D	E
Day-to-day price fluctuations in the value of my investments don't bother me.	A	B	C	D	E
Retirement is more than 10 years away.	A	B	C	D	E
I have enough money set aside for emergencies.	A	B	C	D	E
I'm investing for the long term (longer than five years).	A	B	C	D	E

that your investment's value may fluctuate a bit on the way to a higher return.

If you circled mostly Ds and Es, you're a growth-oriented investor. You probably have high expectations for your investment portfolio, emphasizing capital gains for long-term growth. You're not that interested in generating a steady flow of income, and you're prepared to accept a higher level of risk for the opportunity to earn a higher level of return.

ANOTHER CHECK ON YOUR INVESTMENT PERSONALITY

When you get to chatting about investment goals and investment personality, it often happens that a great disparity arises between what we think we are like and what we're really like. Take the case of Germaine LeGroux:

Germaine walked into her bank ready to do business. She was tired of the low return she was getting on her GIC. She wanted 8 percent, 10 percent, maybe even 12 percent. When the salesperson asked her whether she needed her investment income for her day-to-day needs, she said, "Not really." Could she accept some fluctuations? For a 12-percent return? You betcha! Did she follow the markets closely? Yep, she listened to the news every day. How far away was retirement? Well, she was retired, but all those financial experts said she should still be getting growth, so she was here for growth. Into the stock market she dived by way of an equity mutual fund.

Six months later, the market dipped. Her investment lost 6 percent of its value. She waited. But she stopped being so sure she wanted a 12-percent return. She'd be willing to settle for 7 percent if her investment was a little less shaky. Two weeks later the market dipped again and she lost another 4 percent. She was really worried now. She was counting on this money to see her through retirement. She had at least another 20 years to go. What should she do? Another week of small slides passed, after which her investment was down another 4 percent. That was all she could stand. She sold and stuck her money right back into GICs. She had $12,000 less than when she started. But at least she'd learned her lesson. She was out of the market for *good*!

This story is pretty typical of people who get into growth investments for the wrong reasons and without clearly understanding their own safety needs. People in the investment industry refer to these types of investors as "lambs" (as in "to the slaughter go").

The fact is, Germaine was probably smart to get into equity investing in the first place. With 20 years of retirement to go, she would need some growth to see her to the end. Her mistake was in not understanding her own investment personality before she made her final decision. Her ultimate mistake was getting out when she did. Had she understood her investment personality, she may have been able to predict and thus circumvent her untimely exit from the market.

Following is another test for risk tolerance so you can see how closely your results mirror those from the first test on page 106. If your results are remarkably different, use this test's results. If there is only a slight difference, think about what's different. If there's no difference, congratulations! You've got a good handle on your investment personality.

RATE YOUR RISK TOLERANCE

1. Six months after you buy an equity mutual fund, the value of your investment increases by 20 percent. Your first reaction is to:

   A. Sell it and take your profit.

   B. Hold it, hoping the price goes up even further.

   C. Buy more, since there is real money to be made here.

2. You've bought a stock that's dropped 20 percent of its value in the past two weeks. You:

   A. Sell it and get into something safer.

   B. Hold it, hoping the price goes back up.

   C. Buy more. The lower price is a real deal.

3. You've lost $500 at the track. How much are you willing to risk to get back your $500?

    A. $0   B. $250   C. $500

4. You and two friends are each holding one ticket for a lottery. One of those tickets has won $100,000, but you don't know which. You:

A. Sell your ticket to one of the other guys for $1,000.	B. Agree to split the money three ways.	C. Go for broke. You want the whole $100,000.

5. You're offered an opportunity to invest in a new diamond mine. If the mine is successful, you could get back 50 to 100 times your investment. If it's a dud, your investment would be worthless. There's a one in five chance that the mine will come in. How much would you invest?

A. Nothing	B. Two weeks' salary	C. Six months' salary

6. You've inherited a house that's a wreck but located in a very good part of town. You:

A. Sell it.	B. Put some money into it and then rent it at below-market rates for that area.	C. Tear it down and finance a new home on the property, which you could then sell for a handsome profit.

Give yourself one point for each "A" answer, three points for each "B" answer, and five points for each "C" answer. If you scored...

- 13 points or less, you're pretty conservative. You're uncomfortable with risk and stick with the investments you know well.

- 14-23 points, you're balanced. You're willing to take calculated risks, but like to balance those risks with some safer investments.

- 24 points or more, you're quite aggressive. You're probably very comfortable with high degrees of risk when there are potentially higher returns.

If you find you are a little shy of the stock market, or you rank as pretty conservative but decide to go into the market anyway, get yourself a buddy (preferably a financial adviser) who can hold your hand through the rough spots. A knowledgeable adviser will be able to remind you of your initial objectives and reassure you of what is happening so you don't make the fatal leap out of the market at just the wrong time.

WHAT IS A DISCOUNT BROKERAGE SERVICE?

A discount brokerage service allows you to purchase and sell investments while paying commissions that are far below those of a full-service brokerage. In fact, you can save more than 80 percent on commissions by using a discount broker. If you don't need the advice of a full-service broker, consider using a discount brokerage service to save, save, save!

Whenever you buy securities — inside or outside an RRSP — you'll often incur brokerage commissions. If you contribute cash to your plan and use that cash to buy securities, your RRSP will have to pay the commission, reducing your overall return. To maximize the return within your RRSP, you may be better off buying those securities outside your RRSP (and paying the commission outside the plan), and then contributing the actual securities to your plan as an annual contribution.

Keep in mind that if you transfer a security to your

RRSP immediately after you buy it, you may incur a loss that Revenue Canada will not recognize for tax purposes. Wait till the security increases in value before you contribute it to your RRSP.

HOW DOES DEPOSIT INSURANCE WORK?

The Canada Deposit Insurance Corporation (CDIC) was established in 1967 by the Canada Deposit Insurance Corporation Act. CDIC's primary objective is to provide insurance against the loss of deposits made by consumers with member firms. Not everyone can be a member; only banks, trust companies, and loan companies can apply for CDIC coverage. Credit unions and caisses populaires have separate insurance. Deposit insurance premiums are paid by the member financial institution, so there is no direct cost to you, the depositor.

Quebec has a deposit insurance plan of its own. The Quebec Deposit Insurance Board (QDIB) insures deposits made in Quebec for provincially incorporated members. Deposits made outside Quebec are insured by CDIC even if the deposit is made with a provincially incorporated member. There is no overlap in the coverage offered by the two insurers.

The overall total deposits covered for CDIC/QDIB purposes for each individual account-holder is $60,000 for unregistered deposits. This maximum covers both the original deposit and any interest earned. Joint deposits are covered separately up to a maximum of $60,000. Of course, you don't have to be married to be a joint depositor. Any joint relationship, such as two sisters, or a father and a son, can qualify for joint coverage. As well, qualifying registered assets — RRSP and RRIF — are covered separately to a maximum of $60,000.

Many financial institutions are now set up as more than one company, with each company insured separately for deposit insurance purposes. This means that you can effectively double or even triple the deposit insurance available on certain types of investments. So check to see what your financial institution offers in terms of deposit insurance coverage.

Whether or not you reside in Canada, as long as the transactions are carried out in Canadian funds and are eligible with regard to terms and amounts, they will be covered by CDIC/QDIB.

WHICH FINANCIAL PRODUCTS ARE COVERED BY DEPOSIT INSURANCE?

Financial products covered by deposit insurance include:
- all Canadian-dollar personal savings and chequing accounts
- all Canadian-dollar business chequing accounts
- unregistered term deposits/GICs — demand, short-term and long-term
- RRSPs: demand accounts and term deposits/GICs
- RRIFs: demand accounts and term deposits/GICs
- Ontario home ownership savings plan (OHOSP)
- Guaranteed investment accounts (GIAs) — in Canadian dollars
- money paid for drafts, certified drafts or cheques, and money orders that have not yet been cashed.

Financial products *not* covered by deposit insurance include:
- all U.S.-dollar personal savings and chequing accounts
- all U.S.-dollar business chequing accounts
- Guaranteed investment accounts (GIAs) — in U.S. dollars
- all mutual funds (unregistered, RRSP and RRIF)
- Treasury bills and Canada Savings Bonds (however, these are guaranteed by the federal government)
- contents of safety deposit boxes
- stocks, bonds
- debentures or letters of credit.

IS THERE COVERAGE BEYOND CDIC?

Often people read about investments or institutions that aren't covered by CDIC and they panic. But they shouldn't. There are other forms of protection that exist to cover these types of investments or institutions. For example, although government bonds and T-bills aren't insured by CDIC, the government covers them (though it isn't unheard of for governments to go broke).

Retirement savings held within an insurance company are covered by the Canadian Life & Health Insurance Compensation Corp (known as CompCorp). CompCorp covers all RRSP investments held by insurance companies up to $60,000 regardless of the term of the investment. You can contact CompCorp at 1-800-268-8099.

Stocks, bonds, mutual funds, and other products sold through brokerage companies are covered by the Canadian Investor Protection Fund (CIPF). Your registered and unregistered assets are covered separately, each insured for up to $60,000 in cash and $500,000 in securities or other instruments. So if your broker takes off to Australia with your shares in The-Sky's-The-Limit Corp, don't worry. CIPF will cover it. You can contact CIPF at (416) 866-8366.

If you have your money in a credit union, you're protected. Credit unions provide deposit and RRSP insurance. Since credit unions are provincially regulated, coverage differs from one place to the next, so call for the specifics. The Toronto-based Credit Union Central of Canada oversees all of Canada's credit unions, with the exception of Quebec, and can be reached at (416) 232-1262. In Quebec, call the Quebec Deposit Insurance Board (QDIB) at 1-800-463-5662.

PREAUTHORIZED PURCHASE PLANS

Many people have difficulty paying themselves first. They finance their savings and investment plans with the leftovers from their budgets. Other people find it difficult to set aside the money to invest on a regular basis. The easiest way to make sure you pay yourself first is with an automatic savings/investment program, also referred to as a preauthorized purchase plan.

These plans provide a way for you to contribute regular equal amounts to your investment portfolio. Your account at any major financial institution is automatically debited at regular intervals and the amount invested based on your instructions.

By using a preauthorized purchase plan, small amounts — as low as $25 — can accumulate into a substantial sum. You're never locked in; you can change or cancel the arrangement anytime. Preauthorized purchase plans also offer you an easy and convenient way to take advantage of the benefits of dollar-cost averaging.

WHAT EXACTLY IS DOLLAR-COST AVERAGING?

Dollar-cost averaging is a complex name for a simple investment technique. Rather than accumulating a large sum of money before making an investment, it is wiser to invest small amounts at regular intervals.

Let's say the unit value of a particular mutual fund fluctuated as follows over a 12-month period:

	Unit Value
January	$12.00
February	$13.20
March	$13.40
April	$9.50
May	$9.40
June	$8.60
July	$9.70
August	$10.25
September	$9.35
October	$10.50
November	$12.20
December	$13.00

If you saved $80 a month and invested $960 in this fund in December, you would be paying $13 per unit, so you could buy approximately 73 units. However, if you invested $80 a month, here's how your acquisitions would look:

	Unit Value	Units Purchased
January	$12.00	6.66
February	$13.20	6.06
March	$13.40	5.97
April	$9.50	8.42
May	$9.40	8.51
June	$8.60	9.30
July	$9.70	8.24
August	$10.25	7.80
September	$9.35	8.55
October	$10.50	7.61
November	$12.20	6.55
December	$13.00	6.15

By using the principle of dollar-cost averaging, you'd be able to buy 89.96 units for an average price of $10.92. So by making purchases at regular intervals, you would have 17 units more than if you made your total purchase in December. At December's unit price, that's a return of $221.00 on an initial investment of $960. Pretty good, isn't it? The key is this: the average purchase price is less than market average because you buy more units at a lower price.

Dollar-cost averaging means you don't have to worry about investing at the right time. However, for it to work effectively, you should use it as a long-term strategy — and stick with it! Don't let market performance shake your trust. It's a great system.

HOW CAN I MAKE THE MOST OF MY RETIREMENT INVESTMENTS?

The most important step in managing your investments is to make a plan. It's surprising how many people invest by the seat of their pants. Perhaps they rely on a broker's advice. Maybe they follow the financial press and buy what's hot. Unfortunately, without a specific plan many people may find themselves playing it safe or putting too much money in high-risk investments. Without a specific plan, achieving a retirement income that meets your needs is a hit-or-miss proposition.

You don't have to be a financial whiz to develop a plan. What you have to do is take a good look at your financial goals, and then make some decisions about what you'll have to do to meet those goals. Even if you don't have scads of money to invest, a plan is important.

Remember, planning begins with setting some goals. This may seem like an obvious first step. But do you have a *written* set of goals for your investment portfolio? If you don't, you should. Having looked at what's important to you earlier in this chapter, you should be able to write three or four goals. Typical goals might be:

- To save my maximum RRSP allowable limit each year
- To save an additional 10 percent in unregistered investments
- To pay off my credit card balances over the next six months
- To make one additional mortgage payment each year
- To pay 10 percent off the principal of my mortgage each year
- To invest $200 a month in a mutual fund for my child's/grandchild's education.

Once you've set your goals, the next step is to develop an action plan to meet those goals. In the case of the objective "To make one additional mortgage payment each year," you might choose to put yourself on an accelerated weekly payment plan so that, at the end of the year, you will have made an additional payment against your principal almost painlessly. In the case of saving your maximum RRSP allowable limit, you might choose to use a preauthorized purchase plan, investing a specific amount each month. (That's much easier than coming up with the deposit at the end of the year.)

Since your RRSP will likely be one of the mainstays of your retirement-planning investment portfolio, it's very important that you stay on top of it. Monitor the overall rate of return you're getting, and take a little time each year to evaluate your plan to ensure it's achieving your objectives. A small increase in annual return can mean a significant increase in your RRSP growth over the long term. For example, if you have $50,000 earning 10 percent, after 15 years the plan will be worth approximately $208,000. However, with an annual return of 12 percent, the same RRSP would be worth more than $273,000 at the end of 15 years. That's a big difference, so give your RRSP the attention it deserves.

The most obvious way of maximizing the growth of your RRSP is to make as large a contribution as possible each year. A less obvious way is to make your contribution as early in the year as possible. By contributing to your RRSP at the beginning of the year (in January for that year) as opposed to at the end of the year (in February for the previous year), your RRSP has an additional 12 to 13 months of tax-deferred growth. If you can't come up with your contribution all at once at the beginning of the year, put yourself on a periodic investment plan and make your contributions monthly.

If you can't come up with the money to make a contribution in a year, borrow to contribute. Although the interest on the loan isn't tax deductible, providing you pay your RRSP loan off within one year, the taxes you save and the plan's tax-deferred earnings make borrowing really work to your advantage.

• •

The 1991 changes in RRSP legislation created a new tax break for retirees. Since your RRSP contribution limit is based on your previous year's earned income,

you can make an RRSP contribution during your first
year of retirement based on your last year of working
(providing you're under the age of 69). Make sure
you adjust your income during your first year of
retirement to take advantage of this tax-deferral
opportunity.

If you are over 69, you may still be able to contribute to an RRSP, providing your spouse is under
69. So if you have income that qualifies as "earned
income," and your spouse is younger, take advantage
of your ability to continue making spousal RRSP
contributions.

• •

Another way to maximize your RRSP investments' growth is to
allow them to grow in their tax-sheltered environment for as long as
possible. Therefore, even if you retire before you reach 69, you can
continue to maximize your retirement assets by leaving the money
invested in the RRSP for as long as possible. Use your non-registered
investments as a source of income first. Then, when necessary, take
only as much as you need from your plan each year, leaving the
remaining amount in the plan to continue to grow on a tax-deferred
basis.

• •

If you are more than 15 years from retirement and
do not belong to a defined benefit pension plan, you
may want to consider purposely overcontributing to
your RRSP. Everyone has a lifetime $2,000 overcontri-
bution limit. Providing those funds remain tax-
sheltered for 15 years or more, purposely making an
overcontribution to your plan can work to your
advantage, because income earned on the overcontribution accumulates on a tax-deferred basis. Consider
investing your overcontribution in options that
would, traditionally, be taxed heavily outside the plan
(that is, interest-bearing investments).

• •

When you finally do retire from work, you may receive a retiring allowance. This is often made in recognition of long service, accumulated sick-leave, or a severance if you have been terminated. You can transfer a large portion of your retiring allowance to an RRSP in order to tax-shelter it.

The amount that may be transferred is based on years of service and whether the employer pension plan and deferred profit-sharing plan (DPSP) benefits were made and have vested for those years. The eligible amount is limited to $2,000 for each year of employment plus an additional $1,500 for each year of employment — prior to 1989 — for which employer contributions to a pension plan or DPSP on your behalf were not made or have not vested. For the purpose of calculating retirement allowance rollovers, any part of a calendar year is considered a full year.

> Diane Campbell retired in January 1993. She began working at Easton General Hospital in December 1980. For the first three years that she was with EGH, she was not a member of the pension plan. Diane's maximum retiring allowance eligible for rollover was:

Years of service:	13 x 2,000 =	26,000
Years not vested:	3 x 1,500 =	4,500
Total rollover:	=	$30,500

Your employer will determine the amount that qualifies for the rollover, and if you have the transfer done directly (using a TD2 form, or NRTA1 form if you are a non-resident), no tax will be withheld at source on the funds that have been rolled over. If you receive your retiring allowance directly, you have until 60 days after the end of the year in which the payment is received to contribute the amount allowed to your RRSP. (Note that accumulated vacation pay and pension benefits are not eligible for this rollover.) Your retiring allowance can be transferred only to your own RRSP, not to a spousal plan.

Even after you retire, you can continue to contribute to an RRSP, providing you (or your spouse) are under 69 and have a source of earned income. Note that rental income, alimony, and income stemming from employment such as a disability payment are all forms of earned income.

Since there are hundreds of different types of investments from which you can choose, making a choice is often confusing. (Some of the most frequently used investment options are briefly described in chapter 5.) By sticking to the following basic rules, you can eliminate some of this confusion:

1. Know what you're investing in. Your investment doesn't have to be exotic to do the job. A balanced fund with an annual return of 19 percent is a good investment. If you want to expand your investment horizons, learn all about the investments you're interested in before you buy them. And don't let someone influence you to buy something you don't understand thoroughly. Remember, it's your money and it's your future.

2. Don't gamble. Promises of spectacular rates of return won't pay the rent or put dinner on the table when you're retired. Know the risks involved with each type of investment you're considering. No two investments are exactly the same, so before you invest, investigate.

3. Make regular investments. Regular monthly purchases — and the magic of dollar-cost averaging — will help to even out the highs and lows of the investment marketplace.

4. Know when to buy. There's a right and wrong time to buy most types of investments. For example, buying equity-based investments after the market has been steadily rising for some time may not be prudent. Similarly, when rates are poised to go up, that's not the time to buy bonds.

5. Diversify. Don't put all your eggs in one basket. And don't invest all your money in the Canadian economy. Investment in the world economy will help to reduce your dependence on our economic growth and a sometimes volatile Canadian dollar. It'll also allow you to benefit from strong economic growth in other countries or regions. Remember, you can hold up to 20 percent of your RRSP assets in eligible foreign investments.

On page 121 is a form to help you analyze your current investment mix so you can decide if you're happy with it, or if you want to make some changes.

THE MAGIC OF INCOME-SPLITTING

Let's say you've turned 60 and you've decided to retire. Between your company pension plan and your RRSPs, you and your spouse will have a retirement income of $60,000. However, since you've accumulated all the retirement funds in your hands, you'll also have the privilege of paying all the tax. (The following figures are estimates for demonstration purposes only.)

	Income	**Tax Rate**	**Tax Paid**	**Balance**
1st	$28,000	27%	$7,560	$20,440
Next	$32,000	42%	$13,440	$18,560
Total	$60,000	N/A	$21,000	$39,000

On your total income of $60,000, you'll pay $21,000 in tax, leaving you with only $39,000 in disposable income.

However, if you had made contributions to a spousal RRSP, and you each had an income of $30,000, while you would still have a total income of $60,000, you'd be taxed much differently.

	Income	**Tax Rate**	**Tax Paid**	**Balance**
Yours				
1st	$28,000	27%	$7,560	$20,440
Next	$2,000	42%	$840	$1,160
Your spouse's				
1st	$28,000	27%	$7,560	$20,440
Next	$2,000	42%	$840	$1,160
Total	**$60,000**	**N/A**	**$16,800**	**$43,200**

On your joint total income of $60,000, you would pay $8,400 each in tax, for a total of $16,800. That's $4,200 less in income tax simply because you have two incomes instead of one.

By using a spousal RRSP as an income-splitting vehicle, you can reduce the amount of income tax you will have to pay on the proceeds from the RRSP once you begin taking a retirement income.

REVIEWING YOUR INVESTMENT MIX

List all your investments (both registered and unregistered) below, including their current value and the date they mature (if applicable). Include only your "investment assets" (that is, don't include assets such as real estate).

	Current Value	Percentage of Total Assets
Liquid/Cash Assets		
Chequing/Savings Accounts		
Money Market Funds		
Canada Savings Bonds		
Treasury Bills		
Cashable GICs		
Term Deposits (30–180 days)		
Total:		%
Fixed-Income Assets		
GICs		
Term Deposits (6 mos.–5 yrs.)		
Bonds/Bond Funds		
Mortgages/Mortgage Funds		
Mortgage-Backed Securities		
Preferred Shares		
Dividend Income Funds		
Total:		%
Growth Assets		
Stocks		
Equity Funds		
Industry-Specific Funds		
Real Estate Funds		
Total:		%
Foreign Assets		
Foreign Fixed-Income Funds		
Foreign Equity Funds		
Total:		%
Total of All Investment Assets:		

You and your spouse can mature your plans separately, pay tax on the funds separately, and reduce the overall amount of tax you'll have to pay.

By investing in a spousal RRSP, when you retire, both you and your spouse will be able to claim the pension income tax credit. Since a spousal RRSP can be converted to provide a pension income, you and your spouse would also both be able to claim the $1,000 pension income tax credit. If your spouse did not have a source of pension income, this tax credit may be wasted.

The February 1994 budget has given us yet one more reason to plan to income split in retirement. The age tax credit of $3,482, which saves people 65 and older about $980 a year, is being changed. Until now it has been universally available. However, like many other "universal" benefits, this one is now being means-tested. Starting in 1994, the credit was reduced by 7.5 percent for income over $25,921.

Paula Pritchard is 66 and has a retirement income of $35,000 a year. Since Paula has more than $25,921 in income, a part of her age tax credit will be clawed back. In 1994 her age tax credit will be reduced by 7.5 percent of her income above the cutoff amount:

$$(\$35,000 - \$25,921) \times 7.5\% = \$9,079 \times 7.5\% = \$680.93$$

Therefore, Paula's age tax credit will be reduced from $3,482 to $2,801.07 ($3482 − $680.83). This means that in 1994, Paula will pay approximately $187 more in tax than she used to.

In 1995, the reduction increased to 15 percent so that, according to the finance department, people with an income of $50,000 pay approximately $953 more in tax, and at an income of $75,000 they pay almost $1,000 a year more in taxes.

The threshold for calculating the clawback on the age tax credit will be indexed for inflation. However, this only occurs to the extent that the consumer price index rises by more than three percent. This means the reduction will hit more retirees as years go by.

Income-splitting may also help you avoid the OAS clawback. In 1989 the federal government announced that anyone with retirement income above $53,215 a year must repay part or all of their Old Age Security (OAS). As with the age tax credit, this limit is partially indexed for inflation, with the first three percent of any increase in the consumer price index excluded. This limit is applicable to individuals, and currently there is no family-income provision. So, if your family income is $60,000 based on only your income, a portion of your OAS would be clawed back. However, if you and your spouse each earn an income of $30,000, you'll both be able to keep your full OAS benefits (although you'll lose part of your age tax credit).

There are a number of rules that inhibit income-splitting through the transferring of assets from one spouse to another. For example, if you lend your spouse money or transfer assets to his name, any income earned on those funds/assets will be attributed back to you for tax purposes — so you'll have to pay the tax. Instead of trying to figure out how you can give your spouse the money to invest, restructure the way you finance your family budget. Whichever spouse has the higher income (and, therefore, pays more tax) should pay all the family's expenses. The spouse with the lower income can then use his money for investment purposes. Since the income earned will be taxed in that spouse's hands, the "family" will pay less tax on the investment income.

Interestingly enough, there's no attribution rule associated with money you give your spouse to pay his taxes (go figure!). So the higher-income spouse should gift "tax" money so the lower-income spouse can keep his money for investments; he'll pay tax on the income earned at a lower rate.

To maximize your income-splitting, you may also want to consider splitting your CPP benefits. By doing so, you may be able to even out your incomes, reduce the overall tax paid, and avoid the OAS clawback. See page 31 for more details.

WHAT'S THE BEST WAY TO SAVE ON MY TAXES AFTER I RETIRE?

The single biggest bill most Canadians face each year is their *tax* bill.

In fact, Canadians pay one of the highest levels of tax in the world. And our tax bill has been on the rise. The Fraser Institute calculates that in 1961 the average Canadian paid 34 percent of his income in taxes of one kind or another. By 1993 that figure had risen to 44 percent. It's unlikely we'll see a reversal of this trend, so we need to ensure we're not paying more tax than absolutely necessary.

While some of these ideas have been mentioned before, here's a summary.

1. Once you are 65, make sure you have enough pension income to take advantage of the $1,000 pension income tax credit. Convert a portion of your RRSPs to a RRIF or buy an annuity (with registered or unregistered funds) to qualify for this tax-free income. If you do not have sufficient income to use your credit in total, you can transfer any unused portion of the credit to your spouse.

2. People 65 and older also qualify for the age credit. If one spouse can't use this tax credit fully, the unused portion can be transferred to the other spouse's return.

3. Since the government's broadening of the definition of *disability*, more people now qualify for the disability credit. If you think you may, have your doctor complete the Disability Credit Certificate (Form 2201). For more information, check the rules in the General Tax Guide.

If you find that either you or your spouse can't claim all the tax credits available to you because you don't have enough income, you can transfer some of these credits to the other spouse. The pension income, age, and disability credits all qualify to be transferred. Since this can save you a lot on your taxes, be careful not to overlook it.

4. Claim the GST tax credit. Since your income in retirement will very likely be less than when you were working, you may be eligible for this. In 1993, you were entitled to a GST rebate if your single income was less than $29,901 or if your family income was less than $38,801. Don't assume you won't get it; check it out.

5. Maximize your medical expense credit by having the lower-income spouse claim all medical costs. And remember, private insurance premiums for coverage both inside and outside Canada qualify for the medical tax credit. The expenses you claim may be for *any* 12-month period ending in the tax year for which you're filing, so choose the time frame that gives you the largest claim. And since the credit is based on when expenses are paid (as opposed to when the service is rendered), it may make sense to prepay an upcoming expense to maximize your tax benefit.

6. If you receive a retiring allowance, you can transfer a portion (or perhaps all) of that to your RRSP to maximize the tax deferral on those funds.

7. When you retire, you still have at least one more contribution that can be made to an RRSP (based on your previous year's earned income). Make sure you take advantage of this. If you have eligible earned income and you and/or your spouse is under 69, you can continue making RRSP contributions.

8. If you have any unused deduction room (that is, if you have not claimed all your allowable RRSP deductions), make sure you don't let it go unclaimed — and waste it.

9. If one spouse has dividend income but has little or no other income and therefore cannot claim the dividend tax credit, the dividends can be reported on the other spouse's return. This transfer is particularly beneficial when it reduces the lower-income spouse's income enough, so that the higher-income spouse can claim the spousal tax credit. Since partial claims are not allowed, in most circumstances whenever there is any opportunity to claim the spousal tax credit, all the lower-income spouse's dividend should be claimed.

10. Take advantage of the tax benefits of income-splitting by using a spousal RRSP and, if appropriate, by splitting CPP benefits.

11. Defer tax for as long as possible by first using your unregistered assets to produce an income. Leave your RRSPs intact for as long as possible so they can continue to grow on a tax-sheltered basis.

12. If you have investment income, you can claim a number of expenses against it, including the expense of a safety deposit box and the interest on money borrowed for investment purposes.

13. Let one spouse claim all charitable donations. You get the biggest break when donations exceed $200, as long as both of you have an income. Revenue Canada doesn't care who makes the claim. Just remember that your claims are limited to a maximum of 20 percent of your net income. By claiming all donations made over several years in one year, you'll increase your tax benefit. When you make a donation to a registered charity, you'll receive a federal tax credit of 17 percent on the first $200 and 29 percent for all donations over that. So if you normally make donations of $100 a year, by combining three or more years of contributions, you'll qualify for a larger tax credit.

14. Remit your installment payment on time. As a retiree, you're responsible for getting out tax to Revenue Canada on time. And there can be heavy penalties for failing to follow the tax man's rules. Contact Revenue Canada for the information you need to stay on the tax man's good side.

15. If you have a high retirement income (even after income-splitting), manage your income to benefit from OAS at least once every two years.

16. If you plan to help educate a grandchild or help children buy a home, you may want to consider using an inter-vivos trust. You would be giving a certain amount of money to a beneficiary (while you are still alive), and the return on that money would be earned, and taxed, in the beneficiary's hands.

> When Polly and Matheau Trudell retired, their youngest granddaughter, Katya, was just entering high school. Polly and Matheau wanted to help Katya through university, so they set up an inter-vivos trust with $5,000. The income earned on that $5,000 was taxed in Katya's hands, so each year only a minimal amount of tax had to be paid. Less tax meant Katya's university fund grew

faster than it would have if it had been taxed in her grandparents' hands.

A FINAL WORD ON CHOOSING YOUR INVESTMENTS

There's no sure way to invest big and win big. Successful investing is a little like the tortoise and the hare: slow and steady wins the race. Rather than looking for the big payoff, at this point your objective should be to earn a fair return on your investments without placing yourself, and your long-term income, at risk. This isn't the time to seek aggressive growth in your capital by investing large amounts of money in speculative or highly fluctuating investments. The closer you are to retirement, the more conservative your objectives should be with regard to growth. Your focus should turn to capital preservation, minimizing your taxes and maximizing your income.

As you enter retirement, capital preservation and income become even more important. Once you stop working, it may be impossible to make up capital lost because of an unwise investment choice. And as you progress through retirement, simplification of your investments will become more important. Since your financial health requires a certain amount of attention and effort, you'll need to weigh the work to be done against the effort you must put into the process.

I DON'T HAVE THE EXPERTISE OR ENERGY TO MANAGE MY ASSETS. WHAT CAN I DO?

There are two financial services that may interest you: investment administration (IA) and investment management (IM).

Are you frustrated by having to handle all the paperwork associated with your investments? If you are, investment administration services provided by most trust companies and banks (through their trust arms) may be just what you're looking for. IA is a specialized service that involves all record keeping, reporting, and administration related to your investment portfolio. If you have assets of $200,000 or more to invest, this service will:
- implement your securities transactions — usually through any broker — as you and/or your financial adviser direct

- hold your securities in safekeeping

- provide regular reports on the status of your portfolio, valuations of holdings, and any other information you may need

- collect interest, dividends, or other investment income, crediting these to your specified account on the due date

- complete income tax reporting forms and make remittances on your behalf

- pay your bills and manage your household/personal finances, which may be of particular interest to you if you are out of the country for extended periods.

If you're concerned about ensuring that your investments receive professional attention to protect your capital and give you the income you need to live on, investment management may be the service for you. As with IA, you'll need a minimum of $200,000 to make it worth your while in terms of the fees charged.

Trust advisers help you to establish clear investment objectives. Your investment portfolio is then structured to meet your specific needs. Make sure you have regular meetings and ongoing contact to ensure that strategies are re-evaluated and adjusted to reflect changes in your needs or economic conditions.

Investment management is usually available in two forms: discretionary or non-discretionary. With discretionary IM, trust officers make all the decisions with regard to the day-to-day trading of investments, based on the framework established. This option will suit you if you don't wish to be concerned about the day-to-day management of your assets. With non-discretionary investment management, trust representatives make recommendations, but you have the final word on whether to proceed. This option will suit you if you want to maintain control and wish to approve investment changes before they are made. Fees for both kinds of management are usually the same.

IM offers you the opportunity to create a personally customized asset mix. If you are familiar with mutual funds and how they work, you'll know that people buy mutual funds to achieve the diversification they need with lower dollar investments. However, with

$200,000 or more in investable assets, you can build a personalized portfolio of diversified assets designed and managed for you.

You may think that you'd have to pay more for a customized portfolio. Not necessarily so. As you know, every mutual fund has an administration fee that is charged directly against the fund. This fee can range to upward of two percent. IM fees are charged on a sliding scale and are often comparable with the fees charged on a mutual fund. However, for a comparable fee, you receive much more: a higher level of personalized service, a customized portfolio designed to meet your specific needs, and the investment power of all your assets working together to achieve your specific objectives. Investment management also makes it easy for you to track your investment activities, by consolidating them. And you'll receive one statement that clearly shows the investments you are holding, how those investments are changing, and the return you're earning.

Now, doesn't having your own personal money manager sound like a good idea?

6 A QUICK LOOK AT INVESTMENT OPTIONS

There are hundreds of different investment options from which you can choose when building your retirement nest egg. The following descriptions have been provided to introduce you in a general way to the most often used investments. If you actually decide to use any of these options for the first time, make sure you follow rule #1 from chapter 5 (page 119):

> *Know what you're investing in. If you want to expand your investment horizons, learn all about the investments you're interested in before you buy them.*

WHAT ARE GUARANTEED INVESTMENT CERTIFICATES (GICS)?

A GIC or term deposit is most simply described as a deposit made for a fixed term at a guaranteed rate. Some people refer to these types of investments as either GICs or term deposits, using the terms interchangeably. Others see term deposits as short-term (under one year) investments, while they see GICs as being long-term (over one year). Some people see GICs as non-redeemable and term deposits as being cashable whenever they need the money, usually with an interest penalty.

People who buy GICs tend to be more conservative investors who are concerned with the security of their savings; they do not want to bear any of the risk usually associated with investments such as stocks and bonds. Retirees, for example, often depend on the interest from their GICs for regular income.

There are a number of special features you should look at when shopping for a GIC. For example, while some financial institutions restrict their maturity dates to annual or semi-annual intervals, with others you have the flexibility to choose the exact date you want your investment to mature, from 30 days or five years (although it usually matures on a business day). Many institutions offer bonus interest to individuals over 60. And some allow their GICs to be transferred or cashed in prior to maturity.

There are a number of factors that have to be considered when buying GICs. First we will look at the relationship between rate and term. The term of a GIC is the length of time the money is invested. As the terms of GICs vary, so do the rates of interest paid. This relationship is not fixed, but reflects current market conditions as well as financial analysts' projections for future interest rates. Generally, the longer the money is on deposit, the higher the interest you'll earn. A consistently increasing spread between the one-year term and the five-year term reflects a very stable market with a likelihood of increasing rates. This is referred to as a *normal* yield curve. With a normal yield curve, the longer the term of the deposit, the higher the rate of interest earned. Sometimes the economy goes through periods when long-term rates are lower than short-term rates. This is referred to as an *inverted* yield curve. With an inverted yield curve, the rate paid on longer terms (the five-year term), is lower than that paid on shorter terms (one to four years). Sometimes the situation arises where there is little difference in the rate paid whether the investment is for one year or for five. When interest rates paid remain the same despite the length of the deposit, this is referred to as a *flat* yield curve.

The establishment of rates is far more sophisticated than this simple explanation. However, this explanation has been provided to give you an insight into the different relationships that exist between term and rate.

You should also know that rates are decided weekly (or even daily), so you should check around before deciding where to make your purchase.

In deciding on a term, you have to consider the "risk" associated with GICs. Yes, contrary to popular belief, there is a level of risk associated with this type of investment. One risk is that interest rates will rise and you will be locked in to a lower rate. Alternatively, if you've invested at a high rate, the risk then becomes that interest rates will be significantly lower when it comes time to renew.

We saw this happen to people who chose to invest in five-year GICs in 1988. When it came time to renew their investments in 1993, the best they could do was about four percent. That meant a six- to eight-percent drop in return — rough for people living on a fixed income.

Another risk you'll have to face is the risk that the interest rate you lock in at won't provide a sufficient hedge against inflation. Here's how inflation works against you:

> Caroline Terris invested $10,000 in a term deposit paying 4.25 percent. During the second year of her five-year term, inflation rose to 5 percent. While Caroline's term deposit will earn $425 in interest each year (assuming it isn't compounding), she'll have to pay tax on that interest. Assuming a relatively low rate of tax because she's retired and has a lower income — let's say 20 percent, or $85 — Caroline's net return is $340. But that's less than she needs to keep pace with inflation. To be able to have the same purchasing power, she would have had to earn $500 net of taxes — or a return of 6.25 percent.

HOW CAN I MINIMIZE MY EXPOSURE TO INTEREST RATE RISK?

That's easy. Simply stagger your maturities. For example, rather than investing $30,000 in a five-year GIC, invest $6,000 in a one-year term, $6,000 in a two-year term, and so on. That way, since you have some money maturing each year, you'll reduce your exposure to significant changes in interest rates. When rates are particularly low, only some of your money will be coming due for renewal. This will average out with periods of higher interest rates.

When buying GICs, follow these steps:

1. Establish the term for your investment. Remember to reduce your interest rate risk by choosing a range of maturities — also referred to as staggering your maturities — so that every year there are some certificates maturing.

2. Confirm that the amount of your investment meets minimum deposit requirements and bonus interest opportunities.

3. Discuss interest income payouts in terms of your need for regular income, as well as rates of return available on different interest payment options.

4. Discuss rate of return and how that could be increased by increasing the amount of the investment. Consider consolidating your GIC investments held at other institutions in order to negotiate higher interest rates and to take advantage of bonus interest offered on higher deposits.

WHAT ARE TREASURY BILLS?

These are short-term government debt securities issued in large denominations (usually $25,000 to $50,000) and sold chiefly to large institutional investors. They are sold at a discount and mature at "par." The difference between the issue price and par will be taxed as interest on maturity. Treasury bills, or T-bills, can be purchased for terms of between 30 days and one year. The rate of return is usually higher than the concurrent interest rates being offered at most financial institutions. This makes them attractive as a fixed-term investment for those investors looking for a high level of security.

WHAT IS A MORTGAGE-BACKED SECURITY (MBS)?

An MBS is created when lending institutions pool a number of residential first mortgages and allow a customer to purchase an "undivided interest" in the pool. Undivided interest means that the buyer has a claim on the cash flow, including the principal, interest, prepayments, liquidation, and penalties generated by the mortgages in the pool. The claim a buyer has is proportionate to the percentage of the pool that person owns.

Since they can be sold prior to maturity, MBSs offer a high level of liquidity. However, the selling price is not guaranteed. MBSs, like most fixed-income investments, are interest rate sensitive. If rates go up, the price of the MBS will fall. If rates go down, the amount you can sell your MBS for will rise.

The underlying mortgages in a pool of NHA mortgage-backed securities are insured by the Canada Mortgage and Housing Corporation so that both the principal and interest are fully guaranteed. This adds to the security of the investment because should a mortgage go into default, the recovery by the pool will not be dependent on the sale of the property. For this reason, NHA mortgage-backed securities are ideal for people who want to generate a monthly income. MBSs are available in denominations of $5,000. Tax is payable on the interest portion of the monthly payment you receive, but not on the rest.

When you use an MBS, it's important to remember that a portion of your capital is being repaid to you with each payment you receive. So, when your $5,000 unit eventually matures, you won't receive $5,000 back. And if you've spent the portion of your principal repaid to you each month, your capital will have been reduced. For this reason, you might want to consider reinvesting the capital portion of the money you receive each month. You can use that capital to buy a mutual fund, for example, putting the principles of dollar-cost averaging to work for you.

WHAT IS A BOND?

A bond is a debt security issued by a corporation (or government) to raise funds. It represents a creditor relationship, rather than ownership as is the case with a stock. Most bonds pay a set rate of interest semi-annually for the life of the bond, with the principal due at maturity. Large corporations have found many ways of designing bonds to attract investors while keeping costs in line. These range from mortgage bonds, which corporations issue when they have adequate fixed assets to be pledged, through to debentures, which companies can issue if their financial rating is high enough to allow them to borrow without pledging any assets. As well, when a company does not possess fixed assets or does not wish to pledge against those assets, but is prepared instead to pledge securities, collateral trust bonds are issued. Much of the evaluation criteria for stocks would naturally apply to bonds, with one major exception: with stocks there is generally no top limit on the return generated. With bonds, however, there is a specific amount repaid at maturity and a standard amount of interest paid for the length of term the bond is held.

WHAT ARE CANADA SAVINGS BONDS (CSBS)?

CSBs are high-security bonds sponsored yearly by the government of Canada. They go on sale once a year for two weeks — usually from late October until early November (although rumour has it that the government is thinking of widening the CSB window). They are guaranteed by the government and may be cashed at any time. If they are redeemed during the first three months, no interest is paid. However, bonds redeemed at any time after the first three months pay interest to the end of the previous month. So, the best time to cash CSBs early is at the beginning of a month.

CSBs may be purchased in various denominations: $100, $300, $500, $1,000, $5,000, and $10,000. Since you cannot partially cash a CSB, make sure you buy them in as small denominations as you can so you maintain your flexibility. CSBs normally mature after 10 years. During that 10-year period (or until they are redeemed), the bonds pay interest; no interest is paid after the maturity date. So, if you are holding CSBs that are more than 10 years old, you're not earning any return on those bonds.

If you arrange a loan to finance the purchase of a CSB, the interest you pay on that loan is tax deductible, provided it does not exceed the interest earned on the bond.

WHAT ARE STRIP BONDS?

When investment dealers buy blocks of long-term, high-quality government bonds, detach interest coupons from the bonds, and sell the interest coupons and bond residues separately to investors at a discount, these are referred to as strip (or zero coupon) bonds. The term "strip" is an acronym for "separately traded residual and interest payments." Strip bonds provide an investment vehicle that meets investors' needs for safe, high-yield, fixed-income investments that offer automatic reinvestment of interest. Often referred to as TIGRs (term investment growth receipts) or sentinels, these are secure investments that avoid the reinvesting of small amounts of semi-annual earned interest. With a strip bond, you know exactly what the yield will be on your investment at the time of purchase. Maturity dates range from 60 days to 20 years.

While there is a secondary market for the liquidation of these investments, there are a few points that should be noted. If the interest rate at the time of purchase is higher than the current rate, it will be easy to sell the strip bond. However, if the interest rate is lower than the current rate, there is less likely to be a market for this investment. It will probably have to be held until maturity (or until interest rates fall below the rate guaranteed by the strip bond).

Since strip bonds offer security of principal and guaranteed interest payout, they appeal to people looking for high levels of security with a better return than is available on investments such as GICs. However, that security also has to be further defined. Strip bonds issued by the federal government are very secure. Those issued provincially are less secure and as a compensating factor offer a higher rate of interest. With strip bonds there is frequently a long period between purchase date and maturity date. Since accrued interest income must be reported every year, tax is paid on the income before it is received. For this reason, strip bonds are an ideal RRSP investment.

WHAT ARE SHARES?

Common shares represent equity or ownership in a public or private corporation. Ownership is represented by a stock certificate that indicates the number of shares owned. The price of the share is influenced by several factors:

- the general economic outlook

- investor expectations about how profitable the company will be, which usually translates into demand for the share

- the company's actual financial performance, as well as other developments within the company (for example, a change in a senior officer of the company can have a positive or negative effect on the share's price)

- how successful the industry that the company operates in is overall.

Shares are found in two different classes: common and preferred. While common-share holders have a say in how a company operates, preferred-share holders generally don't have a vote on company affairs. However, preferred shares do come first when it comes to dividend payout time. (Profit made by a company is declared in the form of a dividend of the stock.) And because dividends are taxed more favourably than interest, this makes preferred shares quite attractive to many investors.

MUTUAL FUNDS

Mutual funds originated in Canada in the early 1930s. However, it was not until the 1950s that the popularity of mutual funds began to grow significantly. In the past few years, mutual funds have become so popular that it is now estimated that approximately 24 percent of adult Canadians have invested in them. There are several reasons for this increasing popularity. Mutual funds have consistently outperformed traditional investments such as savings accounts, guaranteed investment certificates (GICs), and Canada Savings Bonds (CSBs) over the long term. Brokers have used mutual funds to attract investors with smaller amounts of investment dollars, and their aggressive "sale" of this investment option has increased customer focus on this product. Many new mutual funds have entered the marketplace and their accompanying advertising has increased customer awareness considerably. There are more mutual funds available now than ever before. Added to this is the fact that people are becoming increasingly sophisticated in managing their money. They also have higher expectations of how their investments should perform. Since the '90s have thus far been a period of extremely low interest rates, mutual funds have seen massive growth as consumers demand higher rates of return without the usual risk associated with direct individual investments such as stocks and/or bonds.

WHAT EXACTLY IS A MUTUAL FUND?

A mutual fund is a large, diversified portfolio of investments made possible by pooling the money of thousands of investors. Mutual funds are managed by professionals, which means that, as an investor, you do not have to be concerned with any investment decision other than the initial decision of which fund to purchase. Fund managers buy and sell investments in the mutual funds (that is, the underlying stocks, bonds, or mortgages), and the investors share in the growth and income generated by the fund. In effect, a mutual fund is owned by the people who have invested in it. Since all the money is pooled together, invested and managed by professionals, mutual funds are sometimes called "pooled," "investment," or "managed" funds.

It is estimated that it would take an investment of approximately $150,000 to develop a diversified portfolio. As well, you would need the expertise to be able to select investments and know when to buy and sell those investments to make a profit. However, mutual funds allow many people to invest relatively small amounts of money. Those individual amounts combine to form a large amount of dollars that can be used to purchase investments. With a mutual fund, customers can take advantage of diversification for as little as $100. Since the funds are managed by professionals, you don't have to be concerned with making the investment decisions.

HOW DO MUTUAL FUNDS WORK?

When you buy a mutual fund, your money is converted into "units." Each unit represents a portion of the mutual fund's total assets. For example, if the current unit value of a mutual fund is $12 and you wish to invest $2,400, you would be able to purchase 200 units of the fund.

The unit price of a mutual fund generally depends on the current market price of the underlying investments such as stocks and bonds. (The only exception to this is a money market fund, the unit value of which is usually fixed.) When the mutual fund holdings change value, the value of the units also changes.

Mutual funds should be considered medium- to long-term investments because unit values may go up or down in the short term. However, in the long run, mutual funds are managed to provide superior gains over time.

A lower unit value can even work to your advantage if the income generated is being reinvested or if you are taking advantage of dollar-cost averaging by making periodic purchases over the long term. The lower the unit price, the greater the number of units that can be purchased. Naturally, it is always in your interest to "buy low and sell high." That's the objective in making any investment: to make a profit.

WHY WOULD I BUY A MUTUAL FUND?

Do you find the concept of investing a little frightening? Many people do. That's why they stick with traditional "safe" alternatives like GICs. But by staying with these tried-and-true investments, you may be doing yourself — and your retirement nest egg — a disservice in terms of the return you're earning. Using mutual funds, you can enter a new world of investing, one that offers the potential for higher return. And because there are almost as many different mutual funds as there are investment objectives, you can choose the funds that best meet your personal safety needs.

Here are some reasons mutual funds are attractive investment alternatives:

- *Professional management.* Most of us lack the experience, train-ing, or time to manage our own portfolios effectively. Since mutual funds are professionally managed, you don't have to be concerned with the day-to-day decisions required to ensure your investment performs well. Knowledgeable professionals with years of experience do the work for you.

- *Investment diversification.* It has been estimated that if you are investing in individual securities, you'll need at least $150,000 to achieve a reasonable level of diversification. Mutual funds, how-ever, let you achieve a satisfactory level of diversification with an investment as small as $50. Mutual funds typically hold a wide variety of investments spread over many instruments, so your return won't be adversely affected by the poor performance of any one instrument.

  For example, if you invest $3,000 in an individual stock that sells for $10 a share, you'll buy 300 shares. If the price of that stock falls to $8 a share, then your initial investment would be worth only $2,400. That's a loss of $600 or 20 percent of the orig-inal investment. And that loss can come very quickly. Individual stocks can fluctuate substantially over short periods of time because of market changes that can be influenced by economic or political events. On the other hand, an investment of $3,000 in an equity mutual fund would purchase units of a fund that had invested in the shares of dozens of different companies. The indi-vidual performance of any one company's shares would not have a severe negative effect on the overall unit value of the mutual fund. Because of this diversification, your exposure to risk is sig-nificantly reduced and, therefore, the potential loss of your initial investment is significantly reduced.

- *Liquidity.* One of the aspects that affect our decisions to invest is the access we will have to our money in the event that we need it quickly. Everyone should have some cash readily available to meet emergency expenses. You might also want to be fairly liquid so that you will be able to quickly move your money into other investments as opportunities arise. Most mutual funds have a fairly high level of liquidity, which means you can cash in on short notice.

- *Wide choice of options.* People often associate mutual funds with equity funds, but in fact there are many more types of funds from which to choose. Mutual funds provide a variety of options ranging from investment in stocks, to investment in bonds and mortgages, to investment in money market vehicles such as treasury bills. You can invest in the Canadian economy, in U.S. funds, or in international funds that allow you to take advantage of the growth in the global economy. You can even invest in industry-specific funds that focus on industries such as precious metals, energy, communications, and the like. And with mutual funds, you can choose the types of investments that not only provide the return for which you are looking, but may also satisfy your need for special tax treatment.

- *Convenience.* Mutual funds are easy to buy and easy to sell, and that makes them a very convenient investment. Many mutual funds also offer preauthorized purchase plans, and most offer automatic reinvestment of income.

- *Potentially higher returns.* Mutual funds offer you the opportunity to enter the investment marketplace to earn potentially higher returns than can be achieved with traditional investments such as GICs. As interest rates have fallen, mutual funds have become more and more popular as an alternative for producing a retirement income. While some people have jumped in, many others have held back because they are wary of the associated risks. However, the fact is that fixed-income funds often outperform interest rates. The trick to using mutual funds successfully is to ensure your investment portfolio has the asset mix that's right for you.

WHAT SHOULD I CONSIDER BEFORE I BUY A MUTUAL FUND?

- Don't be greedy. Typically, very high rates of return are usually associated with the more volatile funds. Your objectives for your RRIF should be to ensure your capital is safe while you earn a steady return that meets your income requirements.

- Your mutual fund purchase should fit in with the other investments (registered and unregistered) that you've made. Once you've determined the investment mix that is appropriate for you (see page 121), stick to it.

- Long-term results are the key to analyzing a mutual fund's performance. Over the short term, almost every mutual fund can claim amazing results — but over the long term, only the best-managed funds stand out. Don't look simply at the average rate of return; you need to see how the fund has performed each year to see whether or not it has consistently met its objectives, so ask to see the fund's *year-over-year returns.*

- Ask how long the fund manager has been with the fund. A mutual fund is only as good as the management applied to its assets. If the fund manager has changed recently, wait a while before you buy, to see how the fund performs under the new manager.

- Minimize the costs of changing your investments by choosing a good fund family. Most fund families allow you to switch from one fund to another without cost so that you an adjust your asset mix as your needs — and economic circumstances — change.

- Look at the real return (the stated return less any commission charged by the fund) generated by the fund before you make a decision. There are plenty of funds out there; some charge a commission and others don't. While you won't pick a mutual fund simply because it is no-load (that is, there's no commission charged), you should consider the cost, over the long term, in paying a load. Take the time to calculate the real return once the commission is accounted for.

Allow a reasonable amount of time for funds to perform. And once you've bought with a specific time frame in mind, stick to your guns. I often meet people who have bought equity funds that may not be performing to their expectations. They may have held the fund for only one or two years, but are seriously considering selling and getting into something else. I'll tell you what I've told them.

Since you've purchased an equity fund (which is considered a long-term investment), you need to give the fund enough time to perform. These funds aren't designed to give you an overnight million — despite the advertised spectacular returns. Rather, equity funds are designed to outperform other types of mutual funds *over the long term* — that's over a 10-year horizon. If you don't have 10 years, stay out of this type of investment.

"But what about the loss I've taken?" they often ask. Well, the fact is, if you buy a mutual fund that goes down in value, you haven't lost anything until you sell the mutual fund. It's the selling of the fund that creates the loss. If you hold the fund and it goes up again, you may break even or make a profit.

Of course, there may be times when a fund just isn't worth holding. You may be stuck with a rotten fund manager, or the industry you invested in may have completely bottomed out. Once you've decided that a fund isn't going to perform over the long term, then you should cut your losses and get into something that will put your money to work for you.

Just because you've finally taken the plunge and invested in a mutual fund doesn't mean you can never go back. If interest rates rise to a level you're comfortable with, you can always switch back to a GIC. In the meantime, widen your perspective a little. Learn all about mutual funds in general, and how diversification can help you achieve your objectives. Call the individual mutual fund companies you're interested in and get information on the year-over-year performance of the fund and the fund manager's track record. Investigate your options, and look for new opportunities. At the very least, aim for a return that allows you to keep your capital intact for as long as possible.

TYPES OF MUTUAL FUNDS

Mutual fund assets have grown from $34 billion in 1989 to over $200 billion in 1996, and new funds are constantly being introduced as mutual fund companies, banks, brokerage houses, and insurance companies fight to capture more of our investment dollars.

Most mutual funds operate in more or less the same way. However, their investment portfolios — the individual investments they hold — are different. Here are the general types of funds available:

Money Market Funds

Money market funds invest in portfolios of money market investments and savings deposits. They provide high levels of interest income without risk to your capital. Investments held can include short-term government bonds, treasury bills, term deposits, GICs, short-term promissory notes, and bankers' acceptances.

Money market funds differ from other types of mutual funds in the way their unit values are set. While the unit values of other funds fluctuate, rising or falling, to provide you with a capital gain or capital loss, the unit value of a money market fund remains fairly constant. The return provided is the income that is paid. Since the unit value seldom fluctuates, there is little possibility that you will lose your initial investment with this type of mutual fund. This is one reason money market funds are so popular.

Money market funds offer you the opportunity to take advantage of investments that, typically, are not available to individual investors or that require large amounts of money. You can also benefit from the economies of scale associated with a mutual fund making the purchase. When purchasing T-bills, for example, the price quoted (described in terms of the return, or yield, you will earn) will vary; the more you invest, the better the price you will be quoted. Since mutual funds can buy T-bills in large quantities, unit holders can earn a higher return (because prices quoted are more favourable for large transactions) than if they tried to buy T-bills directly.

Fixed-Income Funds

Fixed-income funds may invest in portfolios of mortgages, bonds, or preferred shares. Since the interest on a bond or mortgage or a dividend on a preferred share is established at the time it is issued, it is referred to as a fixed-income investment.

The main objective of a dividend income fund is the generation of regular income in the form of dividends. Most of these funds invest in preferred shares, while some invest in a combination of high-quality common shares, as well as holding preferred shares in the portfolio.

Mortgage funds hold a portfolio of mortgages, usually first mortgages on residential properties since they are more secure. Fund managers may have a mix of term lengths in the portfolio. They try to vary the mix to take advantage of interest rate trends and invest in a variety of geographical areas. The primary form of return is interest income, with some capital gains possible.

Bond funds hold a combination of bonds — from corporate- to government-issued — in their portfolios. The interest rates of the assets of the fund do not change even if current interest rates change. However, that does not mean that the fund always provides the same rate of income. Fund managers are regularly buying and selling the investments in the fund to secure maximum income while preserving capital. Bond funds also offer the potential of capital gains.

Preferred-share funds are usually classified as fixed-income funds. While they represent equity in a company, their primary objective is to provide an income through the dividends they pay.

Fixed-income funds are more stable than equity (or growth) funds. However, the long-term rates of return on fixed-income funds tend to be more modest than those on equity-based funds.

Balanced Funds
The objective of a balanced fund is to achieve both income and capital appreciation. These funds have a mixture of equity, fixed-income, and liquid investments. The equity investments provide the opportunity for growth while the fixed-income and liquid investments provide regular income. Preferred shares are sometimes included to provide additional income.

Balanced funds provide the highest level of diversification because their assets are so widely spread. Fund managers vary the balance between equity and fixed-income investments, depending on market conditions.

For example, in a period of declining equity/stock market conditions, a balanced fund will likely concentrate the majority of its investments in fixed-income securities. Alternatively, if the stock market conditions are strong, the fund will invest in more equities. The result is reduced risk.

Growth Funds

Growth funds invest in stocks or common shares of companies and are often referred to as equity funds. When you purchase a growth fund, you're usually hoping for a significant increase in the value of your investment over the long term. If the unit value goes up and you sell some or all of your units, you'll realize a capital gain. However, if the unit value goes down and you sell some or all of your units, you'll have a capital loss.

Equity funds vary in growth potential and in risk, depending on the specific assets held in their portfolios. They buy shares in stock markets across Canada and around the world. Their unit values are affected by the relative value of the individual shares on the stock exchange, as well as the current strength of the Canadian dollar if the fund holds investments outside Canada. In fact, foreign stocks can be a good investment just because their value may increase due to changes in the Canadian-dollar exchange rates.

International Funds

Some funds invest in securities from a number of different countries or regions of the world to take advantage of different economic conditions. While conditions in one country may be poor, the situation in another may be very healthy. Therefore, these funds concentrate on taking advantage of the global economy. Fund managers work to earn the highest returns possible by diversifying across global markets. When making their decisions, they must also take into account changes in exchange rates.

Real Estate Funds

Real estate funds invest in income-generating commercial and industrial properties. Your return is based on the income the properties produce as well as any capital gains when properties are sold. Real estate funds' unit values are based on the market value of real estate held. Appraisals on the properties held by the fund are done at least once a year, sometimes more frequently, and the unit values are adjusted accordingly. For this reason, real estate funds can be far less liquid than most other forms of mutual funds, the units of which are usually valued daily or weekly. Therefore, this type of mutual fund should only be considered as a long-term investment.

Specialty funds

Specialty funds tend to concentrate their assets in one particular sector of the economy or in one specific country. Some specialize in energy, high technology, telecommunications, pharmaceuticals or precious metals. Others specialize in one country such as Japan or Germany, or in a region such as Asia or Europe. Returns on specialized funds tend to fluctuate considerably from one year to the next. They have the potential for very high capital appreciation, but can also be extremely risky in terms of capital loss. Therefore, these types of funds should only be used as long-term investments.

IS THERE ANY RELATIONSHIP BETWEEN INTEREST RATE CHANGES AND THE PERFORMANCE OF MUTUAL FUNDS?

Depending on the assets held, mutual funds can be affected by changes in interest rates. Fixed-income funds (mortgage and bond funds) are "interest sensitive." Generally, when interest rates go up, the unit values of the interest-sensitive funds will likely decrease. For example, if you buy a bond that pays six percent interest, it gives you a $30 return on a $500 investment. If interest rates go up, the bond is considered less valuable because new bonds are offering a higher rate of interest (more than six percent). The reverse is also true: when interest rates go down, the investment is worth more.

Similarly, if you hold a mortgage at 10 percent and interest rates go down, the mortgage is considered more valuable because new mortgages are offering a lower return. Because these funds are interest sensitive, both the yield and unit price fluctuate based on changes in interest rates.

Bond funds tend to be more interest sensitive than mortgage funds. That's because the longer the term to maturity, the more impact changes in rates have on an investment — rates on longer-term instruments tend to be more volatile than shorter-term rates. Bond funds may hold bonds that do not mature for 10 or 15 years. On the other hand, the maximum term for a mortgage is usually five years. As a result, bond funds react more strongly to changes in interest rates than do mortgage funds.

WHAT IS A PROSPECTUS?

It's a document that contains information about:
- the fund's investment objectives, policies, and restrictions;
- the people responsible for the management of the fund's assets;
- how income is distributed;
- costs charged to the fund;
- the purchaser's statutory rights;
- taxation issue and risk factors.

Mutual fund sellers must provide you with a copy of the prospectus (or simplified prospectus), as well as the annual audited and most recent interim unaudited financial reports. You can also request a copy of the annual information form (AIP). This is the document from which the simplified prospectus is compiled, and together these two documents make up part of the permanent information record for the fund. Take the time to read the simplified prospectus before you make your final decision.

BORROWING TO BUY A MUTUAL FUND

When people borrow in order to purchase a mutual fund, this is known as leveraging. People leverage for a number of reasons. For example, they may currently have insufficient funds but are expecting their circumstances to change. Whatever the circumstances, whenever you leverage the purchase of a mutual fund, you should be aware that this involves a higher level of risk than using cash resources. You will be liable for any shortfalls between the market value of the mutual funds you buy and the amount owed under the loan agreement. For example, if you borrow $5,000 to purchase $10,000 worth of mutual funds and the unit value of the mutual funds goes down, you will still be responsible for repayment of the total loan, along with all interest, regardless of the current value of the mutual fund units.

Under normal circumstances, you can usually borrow up to 50 percent of the value of the growth funds, and an even higher percentage on income-oriented funds. The interest paid on an investment loan (such as a loan to buy *unregistered* mutual fund units) is tax deductible.

WHAT IS THE FUND'S VALUATION DATE?

The valuation date is the date on which the value of the fund is established. Many funds are valued weekly as of the last business day of the week. Others are valued each business day.

On the valuation date, the net asset value (NAV) of the units is set. The NAV of the units is equal to the NAV of the total fund divided by the total units outstanding.

WHAT DOES IT COST TO BUY A MUTUAL FUND?

There are a variety of costs associated with purchasing, holding, and selling mutual funds. Not all funds levy the same types of charges, nor do they all charge the same fee for similar services.

A number of mutual funds charge a sales fee, referred to as a "commission," or "load," on the sale of the units of their funds. This acquisition fee is referred to by a number of different names, depending on when the sales fee is charged. Some funds have an initial sales charge, referred to as a front-end load, or an "in," which is charged on the amount originally invested. This fee can be as high as nine percent, and is usually negotiable depending on the amount being invested. Some funds charge a redemption fee, referred to as a back-end load, or an "out," and this is payable when the units of a fund are redeemed, or sold.

A redemption fee may be calculated on the initial purchase cost, or it may be calculated on the value of the investment when it is sold, which, of course, may be much higher. However, most redemption fees are usually designed to reduce to zero after the fund has been held for a specific number of years, typically five to six years. That's one good reason mutual funds should be viewed as a long-term investment. Level loads require that the commission paid is spaced evenly over the time you own the fund.

Mutual funds that charge no commission to buy or sell the units are referred to as no-load funds. This means that there is no cost to you to buy or sell the units or transfer between funds in the same family. This also means that every dollar you invest goes to work to produce a return.

Commissions paid on the purchase or sale of a mutual fund can have a significant impact on the return earned on the investment.

Freda Frueman decided to invest $3,500 in a front-end-loaded mutual fund that had a commission of nine percent. Of her initial investment, $315 went to pay the front-end load. Because commissions are taken directly from the amount being invested, Ms. Frueman really invested only $3,185 in the fund itself. That's a considerable reduction in the initial investment.

Had Ms. Frueman decided to invest in a no-load fund, all of her money would have been used to purchase units of the mutual fund. That means that an additional $315 would have been invested and working to meet her financial objectives.

Two years ago Bruce Dobie decided to invest $10,000 in a back-end-loaded mutual fund. The commission payable upon the sale of the mutual fund is three percent of the value of the investment if the fund is sold within the first three years. However, Mr. Dobie recently lost his job and needs the money now, so he has decided to sell his units in the fund. The return generated on this mutual fund per year was approximately 13 percent and the value of the investment at the time of sale is $12,769. Therefore, his cost to sell the fund is $383.07, for a net return of $12,385.93.

Had Mr. Dobie invested in a no-load fund, all of the return generated would have been his to do with as he pleased. That would have resulted in a net profit of $2,769 instead of only $2,385.93 — or an additional $383.07.

Of course the performance of the fund itself must also be considered when choosing an investment option. Your decision should not be based solely on whether the fund has a load or not. However, it should be part of your consideration, because with even a slightly lower rate of return, the real return on a no-load fund many still be higher than on a loaded fund.

While some funds do not charge a commission, they may instead charge a set-up fee. Others charge transfer fees for the privilege of transferring from one fund to another within the same "group" or "family" of funds. Finally, some mutual funds charge a termination fee to cover the expense of administrative work involved in closing an account. These fees can range from $5 to $100.

WHAT IS THE MANAGEMENT (OR ADMINISTRATION) FEE?

All funds charge an annual management fee, sometimes referred to as an administration fee, or a management expense ratio, to pay for the administration, research, and management expenses associated with the fund. This fee ranges from as low as .5 percent to as high as 3 percent or more a year, depending on the amount of research and the types of assets held in the fund. Management fees are usually charged to the total fund and paid directly from the fund.

Management fees can have a significant impact on your return over the long term, since the higher the management fee on a fund, the more that fund must yield to produce the net return desired. For example, let's say both XYZ Fund and 123 Fund grossed 12 percent this year. The management fee on XYZ Fund is one percent, while the management fee on 123 Fund is three percent. Your net return on XYZ Fund would be 11 percent, while your net return on 123 Fund would be nine percent.

It is important that you clarify with a mutual fund seller whether the return being quoted to you is calculated before or after the management fees are taken into account. If it is after, the return being quoted will reflect the net return being generated. Before you make a final decision to buy, check the return you are being quoted with an impartial source. These fees are listed in the monthly performance tables printed in the *Financial Post* and the *Globe and Mail,* and the returns quoted already have these fees factored in. The returns quoted in the sales-pitch and in these newspapers should match.

WHAT'S THE DIFFERENCE BETWEEN "SIMPLE" AND "TOTAL" RATE OF RETURN?

Simple rate of return measures the appreciation or depreciation of the unit value of the fund over the period (typically one year, three months, and year-to-date). The simple rate of return on an equity-based mutual fund unit is calculated by dividing the capital gain/loss realized by the purchase price and multiplying by 100. If, for example, you buy an equity fund for $10 a unit and you sell for $12, then your simple rate of return is:

$$\frac{\$2 \times 100}{\$10} = 20\%$$

Total rate of return measures the annual total return to investors. It includes capital appreciation or depreciation, plus interest, dividend, and capital gain distributions, which are assumed to be reinvested quarterly. The total rate of return on an equity-based mutual fund is calculated by adding together the total dividends paid, plus the capital appreciation (or loss), dividing it by the purchase price, and multiplying it by 100, If, for example, you buy an equity fund for $10 a unit, it pays a dividend of $0.25, and you sell the unit for $12, then your total rate of return would be:

$$\frac{(\$2 + \$.25) \times 100}{\$10} = 22.5\%$$

WHAT IS AVERAGE TERM TO MATURITY?

This term is associated with fixed-income funds such as bond and mortgage funds. It looks at the maturity dates of the underlying investments and produces a weighted average of the number of days or years till the fund's portfolio matures.

ARE MUTUAL FUNDS COVERED BY DEPOSIT INSURANCE?

No. Mutual funds are not deposits, so they cannot be covered by either the Canada Deposit Insurance Corporation or Quebec Deposit Insurance Board. Despite this lack of deposit insurance coverage, several safeguards are in place to protect mutual fund investors.

Regulations require that the money invested in a mutual fund be held in trust by a third party (usually a trust company, bank, or insurance company). This means the mutual fund groups do not own the funds, they simply provide services on behalf of the fund and its investors. In fact, securities regulations prohibit the comingling of the assets of a mutual fund with the assets of the selling institution. Because mutual funds are segregated or are "held in trust," they are not available to the creditors or to the shareholders of the institutions involved with the trusteed mutual funds.

As well, there is a contingency fund in the provinces of Nova Scotia, Quebec, Ontario, and British Columbia to protect mutual fund investors in the event of loss of funds due to fraud, theft, or other dishonest behaviour. The securities commissions are in charge of this fund and are responsible for determining the amount payable after liability insurance and distributor capital have been used. This contingency fund has not been used since its inception in 1960.

Distributors of mutual funds are also required to post bonds as insurance against the loss of money in transit intended for the contribution to and redemption from the mutual funds.

SOME FINAL THOUGHTS

In building a retirement investment portfolio, you really have to take the initiative to learn all you can about the investments you are choosing. The more knowledgeable you are, the more likely you will be to make the right investment decisions. Many financial services firms offer investment and retirement planning seminars — often free. Take advantage of these opportunities to learn.

Remember, too, that the wise investor doesn't put all his or her eggs in one basket. Once you've done your risk profile and understand your investment personality, investigate the alternatives for spreading your assets around. Diversification will help you to not only balance investment risk, but also minimize or eliminate inflation risk.

Keep in mind the impact that both inflation and taxes have on reducing your real return. Work to hold both these monsters at bay. Equity investments will help minimize the impact of inflation, and you can plan tax minimization strategies (such as RRSPs and tax-benefitted forms of income) to increase your real return.

7 YOUR WILL BE DONE

Most people work hard and plan carefully to ensure there'll be enough money to meet their and their family's needs. They save. They invest. They plan for retirement. Often, however, people postpone estate planning and die without leaving a will (referred to as dying "intestate") or without sufficient insurance to meet their family's needs. Some people allow their wills and insurance coverage to become so outdated that they do not adequately provide for all the family changes that have taken place. Often people procrastinate because there is no sense of urgency. We all know that some day we will die, but few of us are willing to accept that the event may happen sooner than later. The resulting delay means many people die without an up-to-date will or adequate insurance, leaving their families to muddle through the chaos.

WHAT EXACTLY IS A WILL?

Wills have existed in one form or another for thousands of years. Historians have found forms of wills dated as early as 2050 BC in Mesopotamia and 1850 BC in Egypt. Of course, back then the rules and format were considerably different. In imperial Rome, for example, you could only make a will if you had immediate family (that is, children, spouse, brothers, sisters, and so on). Where, today, the only legal will is one that is written and that comes into effect on the death of the individual, back then a will was a verbal declaration before a special tribunal with title passing to the beneficiaries when the declaration was made. The modern will, as we know it, came into effect in 1540 AD.

A will is a document prepared by you (you're referred to as the testator), or a lawyer acting on your instructions, stating how you wish to have your assets disposed of after your death. A will can be rewritten or amended at any time and only comes into effect when you die.

The fact that a will only becomes effective at death is important. Some people think that the wishes detailed in their wills will be carried out if they become incapacitated (that is, if they become too ill to carry out their financial responsibilities). Not so. To make provisions for becoming incapacitated, you need to use a power of attorney designed specifically to operate during either mental or physical incapacity (see page 166).

Any number of wills can be made during a lifetime, but in most cases, only the last will is effective.

TYPES OF WILLS

There are three basic types:

- The conventional (English form) will is the most common form. To be valid, it must be in writing (including typewritten), and executed before two witnesses. Each witness should be of the age of majority. The witnesses to the will must sign the document at the same time as you do since the witnesses' signatures indicate that they saw you sign the will.

- A holograph will is one that is entirely handwritten (the will must be in your handwriting) and is dated and signed, *but is not witnessed.* Holograph wills are not valid in all provinces (such as British Columbia, Prince Edward Island, and Nova Scotia). Holograph wills must be presented to the court to prove their authenticity. Take care in choosing to make a holograph will. Sometimes they can create more problems than they actually solve. Vague or confusing wording may lead to questions about your real intent. The result can be delays, litigation, and bad feelings among family members. You're much better off having a will drawn up by a professional.

- A Quebec notarial will is one that is executed by a notary. It must be signed by the testator before two notaries or before a notary and two witnesses, who in turn must sign the will in the testator's presence. The witnesses must be named and described in the will and must be age of majority. A spouse cannot be a witness for her husband, nor can the spouse of the notary drawing up the will, his clerk, or any of his employees act as a witness. Notarial wills are only created in Quebec, where they do not have to be probated. When notarial wills include property situated outside Quebec, they must be probated in the jurisdiction the property is located.

WHAT ASSETS CAN BE PASSED ON WITHOUT A WILL?

Not all your assets will form a part of your estate. Those that do are referred to as "probatable assets." Assets that are not probatable can bypass your will and go directly to the joint owner (usually your spouse) or your beneficiary. This is of particular importance now that the costs of probating a will have risen so much. For example, in 1992 Ontario raised the cost of probate to $5 per $1,000 on the first $50,000, and $15 per $1,000 on remaining probatable assets. With deficits in the stratosphere and provincial governments looking for new ways to generate revenues, it is expected that other provinces will follow suit and jack up the cost of dying.

Even if a will is in good order and uncontested, a period of time will elapse before the assets can be distributed. Only after the claims of the creditors have been sorted out (including legal fees and income taxes) can the remaining assets be distributed according to the will. Assets that can bypass this process become immediately available to beneficiaries. There are three common situations where assets may bypass a will:

- Where a beneficiary is named: most life insurance policies, annu-ities, pension plans, and RRSPs allow for the naming of a beneficiary. On proof of death, the funds are turned over to the beneficiary.

Life insurance can be a very important part of planning your estate. It can be passed directly to beneficiaries without being probated, providing much-needed income while an estate is being settled. Insurance benefits paid to an estate can provide the cash needed to settle liabilities, pay taxes, and meet other cash-flow needs.

- Where property is held in "joint tenancy." For example, a bank account or home where two people are registered as "joint tenants" means that the rights to the property automatically go to the surviving individual.

- Where an inter-vivos trust, or lifetime trust, has been established. If you transfer assets into an irrevocable inter-vivos trust, these assets are no longer owned by you and are not, therefore, probatable.

DOES EVERYONE NEED A WILL?

Almost everyone should have a will. Unfortunately, many people think they don't. Some think their wishes will be carried out by a family member. Others feel they do not have sufficient assets to justify the cost of making a will. And some people simply avoid making a will because their personal circumstances — marriages, divorces, and accumulated children and stepchildren — just seem too complex to unravel.

Few people understand the rules set out by provincial governments, and the implications and costs associated with dying intestate. It is enough to say, however, that if you die without a will, trying to figure out who gets what, and when, is often an unholy mess.

WHAT HAPPENS IF I DIE WITHOUT A WILL?

If you die without a will, or intestate, your estate is distributed according to the laws of the province in which you were domiciled. Your domicile refers to the place you had your chief residence and the intent of remaining for the rest of your life.

> Perry Wiggins lives in Ottawa, Ontario, but works and has an apartment in Montreal, Quebec. Legally Perry is domiciled in Ontario and, therefore, is affected by Ontario provincial legislation if he dies intestate.

If you die intestate, your probatable assets — the property, investments, and personal possessions that you have accumulated and that make up your estate — are frozen until the courts appoint

How Your Assets Will Be Distributed if You Die Without a Will

If You are Survived by:

	Spouse only	Spouse & one child	Spouse & children	Children
Alberta	All to spouse	1st $40,000 to spouse; remaining split equally	1st $40,000 to spouse; 1/3 of remaining to spouse 2/3 split equally between children	All to children
British Columbia	All to spouse	1st $65,000 to spouse; remaining split equally	1st $65,000 to spouse; 1/3 of remaining to spouse 2/3 split equally between children	All to children
Manitoba	All to spouse	All to spouse	All to spouse	All to children
New Brunswick	All to spouse	Belongings to spouse; remaining split equally	Belongings to spouse; 1/3 of remaining to spouse 2/3 split equally between children	All to children
Newfoundland	All to spouse	Split equally	1/3 to spouse 2/3 split equally between children	All to children
Nova Scotia	All to spouse	1st $50,000 to spouse; remaining split equally	1st $50,000 to spouse; 1/3 of remaining to spouse 2/3 split equally between children	All to children
Ontario	All to spouse	1st $75,000 to spouse; remaining split equally	1st $75,000 to spouse; 1/3 of remaining to spouse 2/3 split equally between children	All to children
Prince Edward Island	All to spouse	Split equally	1/3 to spouse 2/3 split equally between children	All to children
Quebec	All to spouse*	1/3 to spouse 2/3 to child	1/3 to spouse 2/3 split equally between children	All to children
Saskatchewan	All to spouse	1st $100,000 to spouse; remaining split equally	1st $100,000 to spouse; 1/3 of remaining to spouse 2/3 split equally between children	All to children

*if you have no other immediate family

an administrator. The administrator is someone who will oversee the sale of the assets and distribution of the estate.

Your funds can be frozen for months while the estate issues are being resolved. These delays often cause financial hardship for surviving family members, who are deprived of the use of those funds during that time.

WHY DO I NEED A WILL?

- To distribute your estate the way you want. With a will, you can specify who gets what and when as opposed to dying intestate and letting provincial legislation make those important decisions. (The chart on page 157 shows graphically how assets are divided if you die without a will.) In some cases, the provincial Family Law Act can override provincial distribution formulas, or even your will. For example, in Ontario, a will cannot override the Family Law Act.

- To appoint an executor. A will lets you choose the best person or company to represent you as executor of your estate.

- To save time and money. A will can minimize delays in the distribution of your estate. If you die without a will and a court appoints an administrator, the administrator's powers only come into effect from the date they are granted by the court. On the other hand, since an executor's powers come from the will, your executor can begin to take action immediately.

- To appoint a guardian for minors. Using a will, you can appoint guardians for your children who are still minors. Without this appointment, the appropriate government agency may become the guardian of your children until an application to the court is made to appoint a relative or other person. That can mean hardship for children and cause disputes within a family.

- To effectively plan your tax situation. By planning the will carefully, you can lessen the impact of income taxes arising on death. By creating trusts, for example, you can effectively split income among various family members. Trusts can be set up for individuals who are mentally incapacitated or beneficiaries who may be financially inexperienced. Without a will, these trusts are not available and children are required to take their share upon reaching the age of majority.

WHO CAN MAKE A WILL?

To make a will, you must:
- be age of majority. One exception to this is people under the age of majority who are married or who have been married.

- have "testamentary capacity." This means that you must have sound mind, memory, and understanding, and must clearly understand that you are making a will that is disposing of your assets. You must understand and recollect the nature of your assets and understand the claims of those you may be excluding from the will.

There are several circumstances that may negate your ability to execute a legal will, if:
- you are under the influence of alcohol or drugs
- undue influence is exerted
- it has been shown that the will was executed under duress or coercion.

WHO SHOULD DRAW UP THE WILL?

While you can draw up your own will, or use a standard form, you shouldn't. Estate law is a complex beast. Let a professional who is familiar with the technical rules and requirements draw up your will so you can be sure it is valid. This professional may be a lawyer or a trust company estate representative. This professional can also help you sort through many of the issues you should think about, so that your real intentions are translated into the legal language required. And if you're well prepared for your meeting (see next page), the process should go smoothly and the cost should be quite manageable.

WHEN SHOULD I MAKE A WILL?

Consider making a will as soon as you begin to accumulate assets. This will ensure that your assets are distributed as you would wish. If you are married, you and your spouse should have your wills drawn up together so that they reflect an integrated estate plan.

Your will may need to be amended or redrawn whenever there are changes in your personal or financial circumstances or if you wish to name new executors or beneficiaries. Review and update your will approximately every three or four years. Wills usually need to be updated when:

- family circumstances change. Weddings, divorces, births, and deaths all result in changes in family structure.

- financial circumstances change. Increases in financial assets may necessitate changes to the will.

- new legislation is implemented. This may have a significant impact on the existing will (for example, Ontario's Family Law Act).

- there are changes in residence. If you change your province of domicile, update your will to ensure compliance with the rules and regulations of your new province of domicile.

PREPARING FOR YOUR WILL MEETING

1. You and your spouse should discuss your financial details together before you go to see a lawyer. You each have a right to know where you stand, and you should both have a say in how your joint assets will be distributed.

2. Make a list of your personal information, including your full legal name, any other names by which you are known, your address, social insurance number, date and place of birth, name and date of birth of spouse and children, marriages (all of them), and existing wills, trusts, and powers of attorney.

3. List your assets, estimating their value. Indicate assets for which a beneficiary designation has been made, or assets that are held in

joint tenancy (since these do not have to be probated). If special bequests are to be made, prepare a list of items to be left to particular individuals or organizations.

4. List your liabilities and any insurance provisions you've made to eliminate those liabilities.

5. Discuss who your executor should be. People you select may choose to decline the task, so be prepared to name alternates.

6. Discuss who you feel would be most appropriate as a guardian for your children.

7. Discuss what special provisions, if necessary, should be made for financially dependent beneficiaries (such as underage children or physically challenged family members).

8. Discuss how your estate will be distributed.
   - Who will be your heirs?
   - When will they receive their bequests — immediately or in the future?
   - How will the bequest be handled if your beneficiary predeceases you?

9. Discuss your burial/cremation/funeral directions.

10. Discuss how your affairs should be handled if you become incapacitated physically and/or mentally.

WHAT IS A CODICIL?

Many changes to a will may be made by the addition of a codicil. A codicil is a signed, dated, and usually witnessed document, and it usually contains a reference to the will to which it is appended. When a will has been amended by a codicil, the will is deemed to have been made at the time the codicil was executed.

REVOKING YOUR WILL

For a will to be revoked by a later will, the later will must contain a specific revocation clause. If it does not, the two wills may stand together and the provisions of the later will may not entirely override the earlier will.

Under the law, if you remarry, your will is automatically revoked unless that will was specifically made in contemplation of marriage. Keep in mind that while marriage revokes a will, divorce does not.

A will may also be revoked by physical destruction. You can burn it, tear it, or destroy it in some other way. However, to be legally revoked, you must have had the intent of revoking the will. (For example, wills accidentally torn are not revoked.)

WHO SHOULD I NAME AS MY EXECUTOR?

When you make your will, one of the first things you have to consider is who you will appoint as your executor. This is the person (or company) who will ensure your wishes are honoured and your instructions are followed. Your executor must be of sound mind and must have obtained age of majority to act. Trust companies are the only organizations eligible to be named as executors.

If you choose to name a friend or family member as executor because he or she is familiar with the personal details of your life, remember that his or her sole appointment can actually create a great deal of stress. Will the person you wish to appoint have the financial or investment knowledge to complete the task? Will he or she be impartial enough to effectively complete the executor's responsibilities? Being an executor can be an extremely time-consuming task. On pages 164 and 165 is a graphic outline of the duties of an executor.

Your spouse may be a good choice if the assets being transferred under the will are relatively uncomplicated. For example, if your estate is made up of some bank accounts, term deposits, a house, an RRSP, and pension benefits, these would not be difficult to administer if it was going outright to the surviving spouse. If the assets are complex, or if there are trusts involved, then a co-executor with knowledge and expertise in the areas of investments and income tax, as well as trust matters and accounting, should be considered.

The appointment of adult children as executor(s), either alone or with the surviving spouse, can have some advantages. If the children are adults and reasonably mature, they will likely have some familiarity with the assets and the ways in which those assets were managed. Again, as in the case of the surviving spouse acting alone, with the child(ren) acting as executor(s), the costs can be kept relatively low. Keep in mind, however, that children may lack the expertise to complete the administration of the estate.

Age is a factor when choosing friends and business associates. A friend may find himself acting as executor at a time when he needs help to manage his own affairs. Also, the possibility exists that the executor may die before you, leaving you without an executor; someone would have to be appointed by the court. Or he may die during the administration period. In this instance, if he was your sole executor, your executor's executor may take on the administration of your estate.

Family lawyers are often seen as a logical choice to be either an executor or co-executor. However, unless your lawyer is familiar with estate administration, he or she may not be equipped to do the job.

If you have a fairly large and/or complex estate, consider a trust company as executor or co-executor. One of the main advantages is that trust companies have the expertise to handle the obligations, and the neutrality to make decisions that affect beneficiaries. Corporate executors are also available 52 weeks of the year, and so your estate administration will not be delayed because of illness, vacation, business commitments, or other preoccupations of an individual executor. As well, trust professionals have a wealth of experience. They've usually handled thousands of estates dealing with the most difficult types of assets and distribution requests. They have the facilities to handle the paperwork, tax returns, valuations, and so forth, which can often be quite intimidating for untrained people.

Generally a limit is set for all executors by the court or under provincial legislation — a maximum of five percent of the probatable assets — and this applies whether the executor is a corporate executor or a lawyer, accountant, or family member. When there are two or more executors, all are entitled to share the fee.

An executor can be a beneficiary. An individual can be a witness and executor. A beneficiary should not also be a witness. (If a beneficiary witnesses the will, the will is still valid, but the gift to the beneficiary will be void.)

THE DUTIES OF AN EXECUTOR

REVIEWS THE WILL

Meets with family/ beneficiaries to discuss will	Meets with lawyer/notary who will deal with legal issues relating to the estate

ARRANGES FOR PROBATE

Arranges for notice to creditors	Provides notice of appointment to banks, etc.	Arranges for bond, if necessary	Arranges for bond, if necessary

ASSEMBLES & INVENTORIES ASSETS

Searches for assets; lists contents of safety deposit boxes	Reviews insurance policies and has them endorsed to estate
Establishes value of assets (arranges appraisals where necessary)	Establishes payments due to estate (i.e., deferred compensation)
Files claims for insurance, pension, and other death benefits	Inspects real estate; reviews leases and mortgages

REVIEWS FINANCIAL RECORDS

Gathers information about deceased's financial affairs; reviews deceased's business interests	Reviews prior year's income tax return; has discussions with lawyers/accountants

ADMINISTERS THE ESTATE

Collects income, receivables, and other money due to the estate

Examines claims against the estate for validity

Obtains court authority to pay support allowance for widow/minors

Defends any lawsuits against the estate

Estimates cash needs for costs of settling estate (legacies, taxes, etc.); determines assets to be sold to raise cash

Files all necessary petitions and accounts required by court through lawyer

REVIEWS NON-PROBATABLE ASSETS*

*While non-probatable assets do not pass through the will, they are an important consideration in settling an estate.

RESPONSIBLE FOR ALL TAXES (INCOME & DEATH)

Files final return; Determines if deferred taxes are outstanding; Determines capital gains/losses applicable

Adopts calendar or fiscal year accounting for estate; files returns during period of administration

Obtains waivers/releases for transfer of assets (i.e., accounts); obtains tax clearance for distribution of personal effects

Files provincial succession duty returns; apportions and collects death taxes from beneficiaries where required

DISTRIBUTES ESTATE

Receives releases from beneficiaries and, where necessary, is discharged from the court

Prepares information for final accounting; shows all assets, income, and disbursements; makes final distribution

KEEP YOUR WILL IN A SAFE PLACE

Once you have made a will, put it in a safe place and make sure your executor and family know of its location. If you appoint a corporate executor, the trust company will likely keep a copy for you.

WHAT IS A POWER OF ATTORNEY?

A power of attorney is a legal document that authorizes another person (or a trust company) to act on your behalf. The most common type of power of attorney deals with property and gives the person you choose to act on your behalf the legal authority to deal with your assets. If you become mentally incapacitated, an "enduring" power of attorney would allow your representative to act for you. Note that it must be "enduring" to be binding if you become mentally incompetent. By executing an enduring power of attorney, you eliminate the likelihood of your family facing a cash-flow crisis because they cannot access your chequing or savings accounts, or liquidate investments in your name in the event that you cannot act on your own behalf. If you become incapacitated without a power of attorney, your family would have to post a security bond and file a management plan before they had the authority to manage your assets.

The person you choose to act for you can be your spouse, another family member, your lawyer, or a trust company. Since the person who has your power of attorney can do anything you can do, you should have implicit trust in this person. If a relationship is shaky, don't test it by adding the burden of a power of attorney to it.

A power of attorney can be "general" or "restricted" in nature. With a general power of attorney, all your assets are covered. With a restricted power of attorney, you set out the specific conditions you want met.

Since a power of attorney is legally binding, consult your lawyer to have one prepared.

In the spring of 1995, Ontario introduced new legislation to allow you to also make your wishes known with regard to medical and non-medical care. While this had been the domain of the "living will" for some time, living wills were not legally binding. The new personal care power of attorneys executed under the Substitutes

Decisions Act are. Ontario now joins British Columbia, Manitoba, Quebec, and Nova Scotia in having passed or having legislation pending to give you the power to choose who speaks for you if you are unable to speak for yourself.

Within the power of attorney for personal care you can appoint someone to make decisions on your behalf and establish in written form your instructions regarding medical treatment and non-medical personal care issues. You can also establish the specific medical treatments you do or do not want, including the specific circumstances in which you want medical treatment to cease.

WHAT IS A LIVING WILL?

In many ways a living will is like a personal care power of attorney. However, unlike a personal care power of attorney, a living will is not legally binding and depends on the willingness of participants to follow the wishes outlined.

Living wills have become very popular as a way of ensuring a timely and dignified death by making your wishes known in terms of a desire for medical intervention. However, in jurisdictions where a legally binding option such as an enduring personal care power of attorney exists, you would be wise to use it instead, to ensure your wishes are carried out.

While Canadian jurisprudence has recognized the right of individuals to determine their own fate, there may still be areas where the laws have not changed. In cases where the next of kin expresses a view that conflicts with the one stated in the living will, the next of kin's preferences are followed, because in areas where new laws have not been passed, the living will carries no legal force. If you intend to use a living will, make sure you discuss this with your family so they are fully aware of your choices. Surprises are hard to deal with at the best of times.

There are two parts to a living will: the proxy and the directives. The proxy is the person you've chosen to act on your behalf. While this is most often a family member, anyone can be your proxy. The directives outline for the proxy the guidelines to be followed, in terms of which medical treatments and procedures you do or don't want.

WHAT IS A TRUST?

A trust is created when one person transfers legal title to property to another person or a trust company with instructions as to how that property is to be used. The person or company to whom the property is transferred is called the trustee. The person who benefits from the trust is called the beneficiary.

Trusts are more common than many people think. Every day hundreds of trusts are created, although not always in a formal sense with written documents.

Here are some examples of trusts:

- when a buyer gives a lawyer money to be used for the purchase of a new house

- when a registered retirement savings plan is opened

- when a grandmother gives a family heirloom to her daughter and tells her to pass it along to her grandchild when she dies

There are two basic types: an inter-vivos, or "living," trust (which can be revocable or irrevocable), and a testamentary trust, which is established under a will and comes into effect following death.

Inter-vivos and testamentary trusts are set up for a variety of reasons. An inter-vivos trust is sometimes used to provide an education fund for children or grandchildren, to split income with adult dependants for tax advantage to the parents, or to support disabled dependants. A testamentary trust may be used to defer the transfer of the asset until a child reaches a specific age (that is, when minors benefit under a will, but the assets are not transferred until the minor is an adult or reaches a specific age). This type of trust can also be used to provide an income for your surviving spouse while preserving the capital for your children.

Once a trust comes into effect, the trustee becomes the legal owner of the property. However, the trustee is required to deal with the property as set out in the trust agreement and provincial law. Trustees are legally obligated to invest and manage the property and to ensure that the income and/or capital is distributed according to the trust agreement. They cannot use the property to benefit themselves in any way unless expressly provided for in the deed or legislation.

168

Trusts are often used as a way to generate tax savings where the beneficiary is 18 or older and is not a spouse.

> Freddy Foxmore's granddaughter, Daphne, was just going
> into university. Mr. Foxmore wanted to help Daphne with
> her tuition and residence costs. However, if Mr. Foxmore
> invested the money and gave the income to Daphne to pay
> her university costs, he would have to pay tax on the income
> earned at his marginal tax rate. Instead, Mr. Foxmore decided
> to set up an inter-vivos trust, with Daphne as the beneficiary.
> He irrevocably gifted his granddaughter the money he would
> have invested, so all interest earned on those funds would
> be earned in Daphne's name. Since Daphne had little or no
> income of her own, she would pay little or no tax on the
> income from the trust.

If you feel you would be able to use an inter-vivos or testamentary trust to your advantage, see professional advice on how to proceed to avoid complications later. Most estate lawyers and trust companies can help.

DO I NEED LIFE INSURANCE?

The term "life insurance" is a misnomer. After all, you're not insuring your *life*, you're insuring the *economic value* of your life, or your ability to earn an income in the future. Whether or not you need to buy life insurance depends on a lot of things, such as:
- how much you currently have in the way of assets
- how much debt you have
- how much your family will need to make ends meet
- whether you're concerned about minimizing the tax man's impact on your estate.

The first thing to consider is why you even need insurance. You may not. However, if your death would cause economic hardship to others, you probably do. As a quick test, read through the following questions. If you answer no to any, you'll likely need some insurance.

Will your estate have sufficient funds to:

- meet your funeral needs?
- pay your accounting, legal, and probate fees?
- pay taxes owing at death?
- provide sufficient income to meet your family's day-to-day needs?
- eliminate any debts you have at death?
- provide for other areas of priority, such as the education of your children/grandchildren?

HOW MUCH INSURANCE WILL I NEED?

Here's a quick formula you can use to calculate how much insurance you'll need:

$$A - (B + C + D + E) = \text{Insurance needed}$$

A = YOUR FAMILY'S **A**SSETS & INCOME
(including existing insurance, a spouse's income, government benefits, pension income, income from investments [e.g., GICs, CSBs, mutual funds], income that could be realized from the sale of assets, etc.)

B = YOUR FAMILY'S MONTHLY **B**UDGET NEEDS
(including shelter, food, and household supplies, clothing, utilities, car maintenance, insurance [home and car], child care, entertainment, etc.)

C = **C**OSTS ASSOCIATED WITH YOUR DEATH
(including funeral expenses, accounting and legal fees, probate costs, estate taxes, etc.)

D = **D**EBTS TO BE PAID OFF
(including credit card balances, mortgages, loans, etc.)

E = **E**XCEPTIONAL EXPENSES
(including educational costs, vacations, major purchases [e.g., new car, medical equipment], etc.)

Begin by calculating the income your family would have, based on the existing income (from pension, spouse's employment, etc.). To that, add the income that would be generated from your assets. For example, if you have $25,000 in GICs at 10 percent, that would generate an annual income of $2,500. And if you have an existing insurance policy that would pay out $100,000, if that money is then invested, earning a return of, let's say, 12 percent, it would provide an annual income of $12,000.

Once you know how much income your family will have, you then have to calculate the expenses it will face. Some of those expenses are one-time costs, such as your funeral or the payoff of existing debt, while others are ongoing, such as monthly expenses and educational costs. The discrepancy between what your family has and what it will need must be covered in some way if you wish to minimize the financial impact of your death. That's where the insurance comes into play.

In deciding whether or not to buy insurance, or how much insurance you should buy, you need to look at each of these areas to analyze its impact on your family.

- **Will your estate have sufficient funds to pay for your funeral?**
  It's surprising how many people make no preparations for their funeral expenses. The more carefully planned this is, prior to your demise, the less stressful the whole episode will be for your family. Remember that funeral costs rise over time, just like everything else, so review your needs from time to time.

- **Will your estate have sufficient funds to pay your accounting, legal, and probate fees?**
  Several costs may be associated with the winding up of your estate. There are ways to minimize or even eliminate these costs, but that requires careful planning and the advice of an estate specialist. If there are costs that must be met, you have to decide if you want those costs paid out of your estate or if you want them covered by insurance so that your estate remains intact for the benefit of your family.

- **Will your estate have sufficient funds to pay the taxes owing at your death?**

  At death, Revenue Canada considers all your assets (except those that pass directly to your spouse) to have been sold. This triggers a capital gain for any increases in the value of your assets. The tax your estate faces can be substantial and may significantly affect what's left for your family. Again, careful planning and sound legal accounting advice can help to minimize the tax man's grab.

- **Will your estate have sufficient funds to provide the income required to meet your family's day-to-day needs?**

  In answering this question, your objective is to ensure that your family can continue the lifestyle to which they have become accustomed. It's pretty tough dealing with the death of a loved one. Adding financial pressure to the picture — expecting your family to struggle to satisfy their day-to-day needs — only worsens the impact of the loss. Therefore, make sure that the death benefit is large enough.

  In the past, by the time we began actively planning our retirement, our children were usually grown and well into the "crumbless kitchen floor" state. Our thoughts were primarily focused on our spouses. But times have changed. With remarriages and second families, the crumbless kitchen floor seems to be a thing of the past. We're having children at later and later stages of life, and not only do we have to plan our retirements, we have to consider the ongoing care and education of our kids.

  Even if you don't have a young family, a retired spouse may be threatened financially because of your death. Often corporate pension plans (and many annuities) pay a reduced income upon the death of the primary pensioner/annuitant. This means your spouse may face financial hardship because of a significantly reduced income. Insurance can eliminate the shortfall in income.

- **Will your estate have sufficient funds to eliminate any debts you have at death?**

  Can you imagine the impact on your family when they lose you and their home? Would you want your spouse and children to have to change their lifestyles significantly because they could no longer afford to pay the mortgage on the family home? Or, perhaps because there is significant debt, the majority of your existing insurance and/or assets is used up repaying those debts?

Insurance is one way you can minimize the impact of your debts. Take a look at your mortgage, credit cards, loans, and personal line of credit balances. With sufficient insurance to eliminate those debts, you also eliminate the worry and financial strain on your family. And with those debts eliminated, your family will have fewer monthly commitments to meet, leaving more for their day-to-day living expenses.

- **Will your estate have sufficient funds to provide for such priorities as the education of your children/grandchildren?** Once you've figured out all the other costs you need to address, you may want to consider the "exceptional" costs — those short-term or one-time costs such as education, vacations, or the cost of replacing a big-ticket item such as a car.

WHAT TYPE OF INSURANCE SHOULD I BUY?

Whether you buy "term" insurance or "whole life" insurance will be dependent on two primary factors:
- the amount of insurance you need, and
- how long you need that insurance to be in place.

Term insurance provides protection for a predetermined period of time (perhaps 5, 10, or 20 years) or until a certain age (perhaps 65, 70, or 80). When the term expires, your coverage ends, unless you renew the term. The benefit paid can be level, increasing, or decreasing. Typically, the face value remains level while the premiums increase as the risk of death increases. Sometimes people choose to use "decreasing term" insurance as an alternative to bank-offered mortgage insurance.

Whole life insurance is, as its name suggests, more permanent, remaining in place until death. These policies can be very complicated, and you should seek the advice of an insurance specialist in learning how they work. With most whole life policies, the premium is the same for the life of the policy, so the annual cost can be low if taken early in life (when the risk of death is low), or very high if taken late in life. Most whole life policies have a "reserve," which can be refunded if you cancel the policy before your death. This reserve is referred to as the cash value of the plan. You can also borrow against this cash value at an interest rate set in the policy. However, if you haven't paid it back, the money owed will be deducted from the death benefit.

So, back to the question, "What kind of insurance should I buy?" The best place to start is with the amount of coverage you need. Let's say you'll need $125,000 to pay off your mortgage, $5,000 to cover your funeral expenses, $15,000 to cover legal and accounting bills, and an additional $100,000 to cover the capital gains your estate will be hit with. All told, you'll need about $245,000. Buying a policy with a lower payout clearly won't serve your needs.

The next thing to look at is how long you'll need the coverage. Some of your needs may be short-term. For example, bank-purchased mortgage life insurance or declining term insurance are the most cost-effective ways to cover this debt. On the other hand, the need to meet your funeral expenses and minimize the tax hit on your estate is permanent. So whole life insurance will be your best bet here.

Remember, the premium on your whole life policy will remain the same, while the premium on term insurance will rise each time the policy is renewed. So while the cost of term insurance will appear far less expensive in the early years of a policy (if taken at an early age), you have to look at the long-term costs. Have your insurance salesperson compare the lifetime cost of both types of policies (remember to compare similar features and benefits — apples and apples), and then make your decision.

WHERE SHOULD I BUY MY INSURANCE?

With more than 150 insurance companies in Canada, the answer to this question is shop around. Get lots of quotes, make sure you're comparing apples with apples, and buy the policy that best meets your needs. Resist the urge to overbuy, but don't sell yourself, and your family, short, either. Evaluate your future earning potential and your family's ongoing needs realistically, take inflation into account, and then buy enough insurance to meet your needs.

WHICH INSURANCE OPTIONS SHOULD I CONSIDER?

When deciding which options, or "riders," to add to your policy, remember that each option will increase the cost of your premiums. Here are a few you may be presented with:

- **Waiver of premium**. If you become disabled (sick or injured), this option will waive your premiums but keep your coverage in place. Often this option is of little value because the definition of "disabled" is extremely restrictive, so few people actually qualify. Before you buy this option, make sure the definition of disabled meets your needs. Also, see how the option is priced. If it is not classified by occupation or health, it will be very expensive. Rather than purchasing this option, consider buying disability insurance coverage — which you should have anyway — that makes allowance for maintaining your life insurance premiums.

- **Accidental death benefit**. This is often referred to as "double indemnity," because it doubles the benefit if death is caused by an accident. However, since your family needs a certain level of insurance coverage regardless of *how* you die, double indemnity often creates a false sense of security. Don't be tempted to buy only half as much insurance as you actually need, relying on the fact that if you die it will be by accident. Less than eight percent of deaths among people 25 to 65 are the result of an accident.

- **Guaranteed insurability**. This is a guarantee that in the future you will be able to purchase more insurance at standard rates despite a change in your health. The amount you can buy and when are spelled out in the policy. Your option to purchase additional insurance usually cannot exceed the original face value of the policy. Remember that while you have the option of buying more insurance, you should only do so if your circumstances have changed and you need more insurance.

- **Increasing face value**. This option allows you to increase the benefit of your policy by a set amount each year; your premium increases with each increase in the benefit. Since the increases are provided automatically, you will be assured that your coverage has some inflation protection. And since there is no need for proving your insurability, even if your health circumstances change, you can still benefit from an ever-increasing face value. As well, with a locked-in schedule of premium increases, you can take advantage if rates are competitive, or decline the option if you feel you can arrange separate, less expensive insurance. This rider usually has an annual administrative fee, so it's only economical on larger policies.

- **Insuring the cash value of your plan**. If you chose this option, the death benefit paid will also include the cash value of the plan. This means that the policy provides an increasing benefit over time — good for inflation protection.

IS LIFE INSURANCE CREDITOR-PROOF?

When a spouse or child is named as the beneficiary of a life insurance policy, the money is considered to be held in trust for them. That means it cannot be claimed by creditors. However, if you name your estate as your beneficiary, the policy is not creditor-proof.

YOUR PERSONAL AND FINANCIAL INFORMATION

Photocopy and use the following pages to summarize your personal and financial information and to get your important papers organized. Review this information every six months to ensure your records are always up-to-date.

YOUR PERSONAL AND FINANCIAL INFORMATION

Where Are These Documents Kept?

Birth certificates _____

Children's birth certificates _____

Adoption papers _____

Marriage certificate/contract _____

Divorce papers _____

Citizenship papers _____

Social Insurance card _____

Will

Location _____

Date of last will _____

Lawyer(s) (name & telephone #s) _____

Executor _____

Trustee _____

Power of Attorney (Financial)

Location _____

Date last reviewed _____

Person/people named _____

Power of Attorney (Personal Care)

Location _____

Date last reviewed _____

Person/people named _____

Safety Deposit Box

Location _____

Location of keys _____

Taxes

Accountant (name & telephone #) _____

Income tax returns (last 4 years) _____

Location of current receipts _____

Automobile
Location of registration & licence   _____
Location of keys   _____
Insurance company & policy #   _____

Life Insurance
Company/agent, telephone #   _____
Location of policy   _____
Description of coverage   _____
Beneficiary   _____

Company/agent, telephone #   _____
Location of policy   _____
Description of coverage   _____
Beneficiary   _____

Health & Disability Insurance
Company/agent, telephone #   _____
Location of policy   _____
Description of coverage   _____

Home Insurance
Company/agent, telephone #   _____
Location of policy   _____
Location of appraisals   _____

Employer's Group Insurance
Employer contact, telephone #   _____
Location of policy   _____
Description of coverage   _____
Beneficiary   _____

Credit Cards & Charge Accounts
Company & account number   _____
Company & account number   _____
Company & account number   _____
Company & account number   _____
Company & account number   _____

Loans

Company & account number   _____

Company & account number   _____

Bank Accounts

Location   _____

Account number   _____

Location   _____

Account number   _____

Location   _____

Account number   _____

RRSPs/RRIFs/LIFs

Location   _____

Account number   _____

Beneficiary   _____

Location   _____

Account number   _____

Beneficiary   _____

Location   _____

Account number   _____

Beneficiary   _____

Location   _____

Account number   _____

Beneficiary   _____

Annuities

Company/agent, telephone #   _____

Contract #   _____

Description of coverage   _____

Beneficiary   _____

Company/agent, telephone #   _____

Contract #   _____

Description of coverage   _____

Beneficiary   _____

Investments

Broker's name & telephone # _____

Account number _____

Location of records _____

GIC certificate # _____

Location _____

GIC certificate # _____

Location _____

GIC certificate # _____

Location _____

Canada Savings Bond certificate #s _____

_____

Location of certificates/records _____

Shares, mutual funds owned _____

_____

Location of certificates/records _____

Real Estate

Principal residence (location) _____

Existing mortgage(s)/mortgagor(s) _____

Title held in the name(s) of _____

Location of deed _____

Date purchased/cost _____

Second properties (location) _____

Existing mortgage(s)/mortgagor(s) _____

Title held in the name(s) of _____

Location of deed _____

Date purchased/cost _____

Investment properties (location) _____

Existing mortgage(s)/mortgagor(s) _____

Title held in the name(s) of _____

Location of deed _____

Date purchased/cost _____

Business Interests

Contact _____

Address & telephone # _____

Type of business _____

Location of partnership/
  incorporation documentation _____

Company's lawyer/telephone # _____

Company's accountant/telephone # _____

Business bank account # and location _____

Location of financial records/seal _____

Trust Funds

I am the beneficiary of _____

Contact & telephone # _____

I am the executor/trustee of _____

Pension Income

Employer-plan contact, telephone # _____

Location of policy _____

Description of coverage _____

Employer-plan contact, telephone # _____

Location of policy _____

Description of coverage _____

Funeral Arrangements

Location of cemetery plot _____

Location of deed _____

Details of prepaid funeral expenses _____

Contact & telephone # _____

Location of funeral instructions _____

Funeral instructions:

Additional Notes

_____

_____

_____

_____

IS EVERYTHING IN ORDER?

YES   **NO**

☐   Has your will been reviewed in the past two years?   ☐

☐   Is your will in a place where it will be easily found?   ☐

☐   Are you still a resident of the province in which your
     will was drawn up?   ☐

☐   Have there been any changes in the Income Tax Act or
     family laws in your province since you made your will?   ☐

☐   Is your executor still willing and able to perform his or
     her duties?   ☐

☐   Have you executed a financial power of attorney?   ☐

☐   Have you executed a personal care power of attorney?   ☐

☐   Have you changed your insurance coverage?   ☐

☐   Have you listed all your important information and
     placed it in a convenient place?   ☐

Since your will was made, have you:

YES   **NO**

☐   Married?   ☐

☐   Divorced?   ☐

☐   Separated?   ☐

☐   Been widowed?   ☐

☐   Signed a marriage or co-habitation contract?   ☐

☐   Added dependants (children, grandchildren, parents)?   ☐

☐   Increased or decreased your net worth significantly?   ☐

☐   Acquired new property (second residence, investment property)?   ☐

☐   Received an inheritance?   ☐

☐   Purchased additional insurance?   ☐

8 IMPLEMENTING YOUR RETIREMENT LIFESTYLE

SELLING YOUR HOME

After carefully weighing all the pros and cons, you've decided to sell your home. Before you put the sign on the lawn, make sure that:
- you've determined the real value of your home before setting the sale price. Don't underestimate the value of your property. Look at similar homes for sale in your neighbourhood. Many real estate agents offer free appraisals; make sure there are no strings attached.

- you've chosen the right time to sell. If the real estate market is at an all-time low, it may be worthwhile delaying your decision to sell. Even a five percent increase in price can mean substantial dollars.

- the house is clean and shows well. A fresh coat of paint goes a long way in adding to its sales appeal.

Many people decide to sell their homes and move to a new location in their community. Perhaps they want to maintain their contacts with old friends. Perhaps they want to remain close to their families. Or maybe they have been very active in their communities and want to keep up those activities. Regardless of the reason, you shouldn't minimize the impact of the move. Even a small change in distance can disrupt routines. You may no longer be on the drive-by for your car pool to the recreation centre. You may have to learn new bus routes. Moving is also very tiring, and can be expensive. Plan ahead for your move, get help from friends and family, and make sure it's in your budget.

People who decide to spend half the year in one place and the other half in another have their own special considerations to deal with. If you've been farsighted and purchased a home elsewhere, you may simply have to pack enough for the trip. If you haven't yet decided where you'll live (whether part-time or full-time), proceed carefully.

MOVING TO A NEW LAND

Moving away with high expectations for retirement can end in severe disappointment. Can you really cut yourself off from family, friends, and familiar places and activities? Are you being realistic in your expectations about the new location? Find out if life will really be as you imagine it. Get lots of information on the area. Think about how a change in climate (higher temperatures, humidity, more rain) may affect your lifestyle. Will you be able to afford to do the things you are looking forward to doing in retirement? Will it be easy to make friends? Will you like living in a mobile home?

Test your new location before you make the final leap. Perhaps you can sublet an apartment for a few months to see what the area will be like to *live* in. I stress *live*, because often people make their decision to move based on their holiday experiences. Visiting a place for weeks can be very different from living there for months. Before you sink money into a permanent place, try it on and see how it feels first.

Another good idea is to subscribe to local papers so you can follow local events and get some sort of feel for the community. Write to the local government agencies to get information on housing and taxes, as well as any special seniors programs. Local chambers of commerce can provide useful information about the community. If you have special areas of interest, mention these when you write, and ask for help in finding people with similar interests.

If you decide to live, even part-time, in a foreign country, you'll have to consider:

- **The legal ramifications**. Some countries will allow you to retain Canadian citizenship. However, you may be taxed according to the regulations of your adopted country. And you will most certainly be subject to the laws of the land. Make sure you know what you're getting into.

  If you think that living only part-time in a foreign country will protect you from these ramifications, consider the current rules for the United States. The IRS test for residency is based on a weighted average of the number of days you are physically in the U.S. over the most recent three-year period. If you are a resident for 123 days (that's just four months) in each of the three years, you'll be considered a U.S. resident (for tax purposes).

Now it just so happens that Canada and the U.S. have a tax treaty that allows people with a closer connection to Canada to be taxed as Canadian residents only. However, you must notify the IRS of your "closer connection" to Canada to be exempted from U.S. tax.

- -

Keep in mind that when you change residency, there are inherent tax implications. For example, if you become a non-resident of Canada, Revenue Canada will say that you have disposed of all your capital property (with some exceptions) at fair market value. So you may have a capital gain or loss. You can elect for the deemed distribution rules not to apply, and this will defer tax until the assets are actually sold. However, you'll likely have to post some security that the tax man finds acceptable (for example, a letter of credit). Check with an accountant before you do anything that might jeopardize your residency standing.

- -

- **The total cost**. While living expenses may be lower in another country, other expenses, such as health care, may be considerably higher. Weigh the total cost. If you give up Canadian residency (refer to Income Tax Bulletin #IT221R2 for rules concerning residency in Canada), you'll automatically lose your provincial health coverage. Also, don't forget to figure in the cost of exchange on your Canadian dollars. Will your money go as far? Farther?

- **The environment**. Make sure you agree with the climate, flora, and fauna of the area you plan to live in. If you don't like bugs, a tropical climate may not be for you.

- **The economic and political climate**. Sure, some countries look really appealing from the outside. Make sure you carefully research any country you're considering as a new home. Beware of countries that are economically or politically unstable. If you take your assets there and things worsen, you could end up losing everything.

- **The language**. If you think it's tough to adapt to a new neighbourhood, think what it's like when you don't speak the language. Don't underestimate what a barrier this can be. And if only one of you speaks the language, you may find yourself living in hell, either because you're totally isolated or because you are called on constantly as interpreter. Don't say I didn't warn ya!

- **How your pension will be affected by your move to another country**. For example, if you want to keep receiving OAS, you must meet Canadian residency requirements. Talk to someone at the OAS office before you make your final decision.

- **How your estate will be taxed**. Unlike Canada, some countries such as the U.S. tax your estate upon your death. Your estate could end up paying 10 to 50 percent in death taxes. There are a number of things you can do to minimize this tax, the first of which is to consult an accountant!

TAX, NON-RESIDENCY, AND YOUR RRSP

If you leave Canada and make cash withdrawals from your RRSP, you'll pay withholding tax at the rate of 25 percent. If, instead, you mature your RRSP and you have a retirement income from a RRIF or annuity, you may pay substantially less withholding tax. For example, since Canada and the U.S. have a special tax treaty, your withholding tax would only be 15 percent.

Generally there's no benefit to collapsing your RRSP if you are moving to a low-tax country such as the U.S. You'll usually receive retirement income with less tax if you leave your RRSPs intact and convert to a retirement-income option when you reach 69.

You must make an election to ensure income earned in your RRSP isn't taxed in the U.S. until it is actually received; so, see an accountant. Not only will this election serve to defer tax, it will also let you use your foreign tax credits for Canadian withholding tax to minimize U.S. tax that will have to be paid.

· ·

U.S. tax on income from a registered pension plan is usually higher than on income from an annuity or a RRIF. One way to minimize this tax is to transfer your company pension plan benefits to an RRSP (a locked-in plan will be required) before emigrating. Talk to an accountant so that you minimize your tax both as you leave Canada and in your new country of residence.

· ·

TRAVEL MEDICAL INSURANCE

If you're travelling outside Canada, make sure you buy out-of-country medical insurance. Most provincial plans cover only 25 to 30 percent of the costs of U.S. hospital emergency care. The difference can set you back significantly — and you may never recover financially. There are lots of private medical insurance plans from which you can choose. Prices vary as much as the levels of coverage, so check the policies you're considering very carefully.

· ·

Premiums for travel medical coverage qualify for the medical expenses tax credit, so keep your receipts and remember to claim them.

· ·

Here are some things to consider when evaluating travel medical plans, so that you know you're comparing apples with apples:

- What is the maximum benefit paid? For most plans, the maximum is $1 million. However, some plans offer considerably less coverage.

- How long are you covered? Ensure that you're covered for the full time you're outside Canada. If you think you might extend your visit, make sure the plan will allow you to extend your coverage.

- Does the plan make payment directly, or will it reimburse you? If you have to make the payment and wait for reimbursement, do you have enough saved to cover you?

- How easy is it to contact the insurer? You can usually count on not getting sick between 8 a.m. and 5 p.m., so you need 24-hour-a-day access to help. A toll-free number is very helpful if you need to be referred to a hospital or doctor. It'll also help if the doctor or hospital wishes to confirm your medical coverage.

- Do you have to notify the insurer of a claim within a specific time frame? Some insurers want to be notified within 48 hours. Don't invalidate your coverage by missing this point.

- Do you have an existing medical condition (referred to as a "pre-existing condition") that may not be covered under the plan? If you've been treated for a medical condition within 90 days of your application, this condition may be excluded from coverage. If you are on medication, will that affect your coverage?

One way to save on the cost of travel medical insurance is by choosing a plan with a high deductible. Just as with auto or home insurance, the higher your deductible, the lower your premium. If you have $500 to $1,000 put aside to cover the deductible, you may save as much as 15 percent. With premiums ranging as high as $1,000 or more, this could mean big savings over time.

- Is a managed care system a viable alternative for you? With this option, you are only covered at hospitals that have prearranged agreements with the insurer. Will the coverage provided be the same as with standard plans?

CHOOSING A RETIREMENT COMMUNITY

Retirement communities are designed specifically for retired people. Accommodations usually have a variety of safety features and can be lived in with a minimum amount of maintenance.

Before you make a commitment, arrange to stay for a few weeks in the community. Renting may be a possibility. Or the community management may offer ways for you to "try on" the lifestyle. At the very least, meet some of the residents and try to determine if you will be happy living in the community. Get them to show you around. Talk about the activities they're involved in. Are they your kind of people? Do you find the lifestyle interesting? Do you enjoy interacting with younger people? What are the rules of the community? How will your neighbours feel about your pet tarantula?

THINKING ABOUT A RETIREMENT HOME?

You may be completely comfortable living independently for the majority of your retirement life. However, at some point you may have to consider a move to a retirement home. This is often a decision that carries a lot of resistance for the retiree. And for your children, it can mean a basketful of guilt when the time comes and a decision has to be made. Save some heartache. Think about the circumstances under which you would be willing to enter a retirement home. Make your wishes known to your friends and family. You might even want to put them in writing. Eliminate the guilt and hand-wringing by planning ahead. Explore the options and maintain control. After all, isn't it better that you make the decision than have it made for you?

There are a wide variety of options, ranging from luxury apartment-hotel facilities to full nursing-care facilities. One way to look at the differences is by focusing on the needs to which they cater:

- The first level could be referred to as the home for the healthy. This is a modification of a retirement community. Meals are usually provided and there is lots of opportunity to participate in activities and outings. While you are expected to be healthy, medical facilities of some kind are usually available, and transportation is provided for shopping and the like.

- For the not-so-healthy retiree, the home puts more emphasis on health care. Activities may be more structured, and diet will be more carefully considered and monitored. Both part- and full-time nursing care are provided.

- For the infirm, the primary focus of the retirement or "nursing" home will be on meeting the medical and living needs of the individual. Full-time nursing care is provided. Little or no emphasis is placed on external activities, since the majority of residents cannot participate.

One of the major attractions of living in a retirement home is the opportunity to be with others. Boredom and loneliness can be wicked associates. Often, an elderly family member may live with a son's or daughter's family and still be alone much of the time. Perhaps the other adults in the house work. The grandchildren run off to school and come home after evening activities. Despite the fact that you are living with family, the loneliness isn't reduced; nor is the boredom.

The opportunity to share experiences and make new friends is a primary draw of the retirement home. Being with other people your own age — people who have similar needs — can significantly reduce the stress of trying to keep up. And having several friends will mean less dependency on one or two primary people.

When you begin to consider a retirement home, discuss your selection with your doctor, social worker, or religious leader. Together, with unbiased advice, you can choose the most appropriate option. Once you choose a couple of residences, talk to the administrator and as many of the staff members as possible. Find out how they feel about the residents of the home. Then, talk to the residents. Find out what they think of the staff, the activities, the meals, and the accommodations. Decide if you feel comfortable.

- Is there a garden where you can sit?
- Is the place clean?
- Are the residents friendly?
- What about the staff?
- Can you take some of your own belongings?
- Can a husband and wife share the same room?
- What's the ratio of staff to residents?

- Are private rooms available?
- Are there set visiting hours?
- Can the home cope with your dietary needs?
- What level of medical/nursing care is available?
- What will happen if your health changes and you require more care?

CARRYING ON ALONE

Living alone in retirement is a very real possibility, particularly for women. Picking up the pieces and carrying on alone will be easier if you've restyled your life to take a period alone into account.

First, make sure both partners know how the household functions financially. Initially, it may seem easier to have one person take care of all the details, but you should share this task. The anxieties of having to figure out the finances at a time of emotional readjustment may be too much for a surviving spouse. Instead, each person should participate so that you both feel comfortable with how things work financially.

It is important that survivors avoid making significant decisions during the weeks immediately following the loss of a loved one. Such a loss creates a high level of stress, and the decisions made in response to such a significant change in personal circumstances may not be clearly thought out. Survivors would be better off dealing with only those elements that must be handled, such as the funeral and probating a will.

BEGINNING THE COUNTDOWN

A successful retirement requires a good understanding of what to expect when the magical day — and all the days that follow — finally arrives. It also requires careful planning. Most of what has to be considered has been covered in earlier chapters of this book. On the following pages is a point-form summary you can use as a checklist.

IF YOU ARE 10 YEARS FROM RETIREMENT

❑ Make sure you're actively building your retirement savings. For many people, with children well on their way to independence, financial obligations are fewer and disposable income is higher. Have a plan for how you intend to put that money to use for the future. If you haven't been investing regularly for your retirement, *start now!*

❑ Find out what your OAS and CPP/QPP benefits will be so you can plan your own savings. Ask your employer for details of your company pension plan.

❑ Do a budget for your retirement so that you can work out how much you need to put aside each month to meet your retirement objectives. This includes not only those savings within an RRSP, but also unregistered investments.

❑ Do a current budget, track your cash flow, and see if you can eliminate unnecessary expenditures to increase your retirement nest egg.

❑ Begin paying off your debts. Your objective should be to enter retirement debt free. Find out what options you have for making prepayments against your mortgage so you can have that paid off too.

❑ Review your investment portfolio and make any adjustments necessary to meet your objectives. With 10 years to retirement, you can still participate in long-term, growth-oriented investments. Remember, the closer you get to retirement, the more conservative your investments should be.

❑ Review your existing insurance to see if it meets your needs now and how it will meet your needs in retirement.

❑ Find out which company benefits (insurance, health, etc.) will remain in place once you retire.

☐ Review your will and make any updates necessary. If you don't have a will, make one!

☐ If you have a particularly large estate, seek advice on how you can shift your assets to your heirs with the lowest possible tax impact.

☐ Start restyling your life. The social aspects of retirement are as important as the financial ones. Decide what it is you will like to do in retirement and start practising.

IF YOU ARE 5 YEARS FROM RETIREMENT

☐ Make sure you stay on top of the financial aspects of your retirement plan. Keep an eye on your budget, pay down your debt aggressively, and maximize your registered and unregistered investments.

☐ Set the date for your mortgage-burning party.

☐ Review your housing situation. If you plan to stay in your home, begin making any modifications you feel will be necessary for a comfortable retirement. If you plan to move, begin reviewing your options now.

☐ If you plan to sell your home to finance your retirement, watch the market closely from this point onward.

☐ If you're planning to move to a retirement community or to a new area, start investigating now. Develop a feel for the area. Practise living in the area by taking vacations (extended, if possible) there.

☐ Decide whether you and your spouse will retire at the same time or stagger your retirements. Develop a plan for moving into retirement.

☐ Redo your budget for your retirement and see how close your 10-year projection was. If necessary, increase your savings to bring your expected budget into line.

☐ Review your investment portfolio. With five years to retirement, you might want to consider a move from aggressive growth to more balanced investments.

☐ Begin learning about the retirement-income options available. If interest rates are particularly high and you want to use an annuity, you might consider buying now.

☐ Continue restyling your life. What have you done to make new friends? How will you be spending your retirement time? Do you have a plan?

☐ Discuss how you and your spouse will live together and share your time during retirement. Will he join her Wednesday-evening card game? Will she take up golf? Will he join her on her daily one-hour walk? Will she take up woodworking?

☐ Begin talking about retirement with your children so that they know your plans.

IF YOU ARE 1 YEAR FROM RETIREMENT

☐ Redo your budget for your retirement. At this point you should be aiming for as precise a projection as possible.

☐ If you have not already done so, establish an emergency fund or personal line of credit.

☐ Review your investment portfolio. With this short a time to retirement, your investments should be more conservative.

☐ Consolidate your RRSP holdings so that when it comes time to purchase an annuity or RRIF, all your funds will be in one place. If you have a locked-in RRSP, remember to keep those assets separate from your non-locked-in assets.

☐ Start thinking about when you'll begin drawing CPP.

☐ If you're concerned about not having enough to live on during retirement, now's the time to consider the options.

Start looking for part-time work. You might want to consider acquiring a new skill that will be useful as a source of income during retirement. You might be able to rent a portion of your home to provide some income. Consider all the alternatives.

☐ If you're planning to move, start your housekeeping now. You'll be shocked at just how much stuff you've accumulated. Sell or give away those items you won't need since, in all likelihood, you'll be moving to a smaller home. Take the opportunity to inventory your belongings and then . . .

☐ Review your will and make any changes needed.

IF YOU ARE 3 TO 6 MONTHS FROM RETIREMENT

☐ Consider how you will be generating a retirement income. Remember, you don't have to convert your RRSPs until the end of the year you reach 69. So if you don't need the income from your RRSP, let it keep growing.

☐ Both you and your spouse should make sure you have a source of pension income so that you can take advantage of the $1,000 pension income tax credit.

☐ Recheck your financial information. Review your government and corporate pension benefits. Review your investments. Recheck your retirement budget. Now's the time to get all your ducks in a row!

☐ Do a cash flow for retirement (see page 198). Write in your projected income in the month you will actually receive it. If you have income from sources that pay quarterly (dividends), semi-annually, or annually (interest), you need to know specifically when that money will come in. Similarly, expenses paid quarterly (tax bills), semi-annually, or annually (insurance) also need to be noted. The whole idea is to set up your cash flow so the income is available *when you need it.*

Doing a cash-flow projection will help you to see your income and expense patterns so you can make any adjustments necessary. Remember, too, that some forms of retirement income (such as from a RRIF or LIF) can be flexible so you can arrange to have your retirement income paid out to match your expenses.

☐ Decide when you'll apply for your government pension benefits.

☐ Shop around for medical insurance if it isn't provided during retirement by your employer.

☐ While you're still covered by your company plan, fix everything! Get your teeth checked, and have any work needed done. Get a new pair of glasses. Have a full physical.

PROJECTED CASH FLOW

INCOME	January	February	March	April	May	June
Company Pension						
CPP/OAS						
Employment						
Interest						
Dividends						
Rental Income						
Annuity						
RRIF						
LIF/LRIF						
Other						
Total						

EXPENSES	January	February	March	April	May	June
Monthly						
Quarterly						
Semi-Annual						
Annual						
Unusual						
Total						

PROJECTED CASH FLOW

	July	August	September	October	November	December
INCOME						
Company Pension						
CPP/OAS						
Employment						
Interest						
Dividends						
Rental Income						
Annuity						
RRIF						
LIF/LRIF						
Other						
Total						
EXPENSES						
Monthly						
Quarterly						
Semi-Annual						
Annual						
Unusual						
Total						

A FINAL WORD

I hope you find the information in this book both helpful and useful in restyling for retirement. With some forethought and planning you can make this part of your life "the best time of your life."

Don't let anyone tell you what you should do (as in, "Mom, you shouldn't be doing that!"), what you should wear (unless they, too, are voting for wearing purple with a red hat that doesn't go), or how you should live (as my Mom says, "Don't be so bossy!"). You're in charge of your future — and a wonderful future it will be.

Remember, the sooner you start planning, the more likely you will be to meet your retirement objectives. And the sooner you tell your children about how important planning is for their futures, the sooner they can get started too. If you began planning early in your working life, chances are you'll want your children to benefit from a strategy you found successful. If you've just begun to plan and you're late along the road of life, you'll likely want your kids to benefit from an earlier start. Discuss some of your retirement issues with your family. Give younger members the opportunity to see what's what, to get a good perspective of the types of things they have to think about well before retirement, if they want to have a happy and satisfying *restylement* — just like you.

Good luck and all the best!

G.

INDEX